THE
BOOK

THE
BOOK

ALL YOU
NEED TO
KNOW

HOLLAND E. BYNAM

1603 Capitol Ave., Suite 310 Cheyenne, Wyoming USA 82001
1-888-980-6523 | admin@urlinkpublishing.com

URLink Print and Media is committed to excellence in the publishing industry.

Published in the United States of America

Library of Congress Control Number: 2021908970
ISBN 978-1-64753-794-4 (Paperback)
ISBN 978-1-64753-795-1 (Hardback)
ISBN 978-1-64753-796-8 (Digital)

20.04.21

DEDICATION

To the memory of my mother whose courage, love, rightness, and unselfishness still serve as guiding lights in all I do. Her lessons for living a purposeful life transcend by far all that I have gleaned from the many others I have admired.

To my friends, including a number who have been under my tutelage that have encouraged me to share my ideas, skills, and experiences with forward-thinking individuals involved in a quest to better themselves.

And

Especially to Logan Wallingford, who I consider a great man and dear friend. In addition to having shown himself to be a model for being true to oneself, he has inspired me to continue in my own quest to improve myself and my work. I dedicate this book to him in appreciation for his sensitive and well-placed suggestions concerning the development of this book, and of my soon-to-be-published memoirs, entitled *"An Incredible Journey"* I believe his gracious assistance in these endeavors will cause readers to see the latter book as a dynamic rendition of a life well lived, and this one as useful in providing building blocks for success.

ABOUT THE AUTHOR

Retired Army Colonel Holland E. Bynam, who is also a retired education administrator, could easily boast of his success as a leader, teacher, coordinator, manager, and program developer in both the military and educational worlds. His work in developing training and improvement programs while serving in these arenas has led to the development of an arsenal of success tips that can be used effectively by individuals who are motivated to seek methods for improving themselves. While this book stems from his own successes during two long careers, it is a continuation of his work to promote strategies and useful formats designed to help others in setting themselves apart from their contemporaries.

The Colonel's portfolio of assignments as an educator and leader is extensive. It includes dynamic assignments as commandant of three specialized military schools, and several key educational leadership positions at the university and secondary school levels. He completed his Master of Education degree at his alma mater, Prairie View A&M University; and was lauded for completing these studies with highest honors. His master of Arts degree was awarded at Norfolk State University at the end of his tenure at the university as Professor of Military Science and Tactics. He has been since honored by that university for being the first of its students to complete the requirements for a graduate degree.

His military assignments include key staff positions at every Army level, including the Joint Chiefs of Staff. He commanded unique battalions in Vietnam, Germany, and the United States, and due to his reputation as a highly trained leader, he was selected for a number of special assignments including being commandant of three military schools: the Army's Long Range Patrol School during his first combat tour in Vietnam; the 101st Airborne Division's Replacement Training School during his second tour; and the Swat Training School in his last command assignment where he served as commander of the 5th Special Forces Group. Many consider his assignment as commander of this famous Green Beret organization as the most prestigious assignment an Army colonel could have. After being touted as one of the nation's top colonels in the unconventional warfare field, he retired from active military service in 1983 as a highly decorated officer.

Although his record of service as a warrior and trainer of men separates him from most of his military peers, his achievements at the university and secondary school level have also been notable. His records indicate that his was the largest and one of the finest senior ROTC programs in America while he served as Professor of Military Science at Norfolk State University. It is also notable that the Houston ISD Junior ROTC program became the premier large district program in the nation soon after he became program director, that it held that position nationally during the seven years of his tenure, and that it continues in that position even 5 years after his retirement from the school district. It should be mentioned that on the road to his being selected to be director of his school district's program, he developed a model high school program, designed as served as the coordinator the district's nationally award-winning Career Academy, and served his department in roles as the operations, training, and curriculum supervisor. Prior to this retirement he was awarded The Commendation For Meritorious Service by Houston ISD's Board of Education for his commitment to student achievement.

While it is notable that the programs he developed while serving in all these positions were always award-winning, his present efforts to make inroads in the educational reform movement began after retiring from the secondary school system. His summer university assignments dealing primarily with entering freshmen students, led to his being convinced that the studentbased behavior problems besetting our institutions stem from the students not being successful. He is convinced also that their not being successful stems from their not being given the motivation, nor the tips, strategies, and a plethora of skills needed in order to deal successfully in their schooling and with 21st Century social, economic, and workplace challenges.

To counter these deficiencies the Colonel developed *"The Super Tips For Success Program"* for implementation at the secondary and university levels. He also developed a teacher refresher program, and a manifesto suggesting actions to be taken by parent-teacher associations in urging school boards to enter the education reform conversation. High ranking educators at secondary, university, and state levels, praised these innovative actions, and lauded the colonel's farsightedness. Some of these educators indicated that is success program was the most advanced yet for empowering students, and in recommending that it be made available to wider audiences, urged him to present the program in a format that would appeal to Success Clubs. In doing so, he developed a new set of books for a program entitled, *"All-Around Success In A Nutshell."* These books are advertised on his website, www.allaroundsuccessbook.com.

It has been often said that the Colonel's written works are laden with the sort of thoughts that a mentor would pass on to knowledgeable subject. This is even suggested in the words of the reviewer of his latest work, a book of memoirs entitled *"An Incredible Journey"* After praising the innovative format used in telling a compelling story, the reviewer stated: *"Not only did I find myself immersed in the storyline of this sagaladen epic, at its end I found that I had been more enriched by the content therein, than from any other book I have reviewed."*

While there is no intention to produce a storyline in the present book, the Colonel's focus is in keeping with his theme that much of what people need to know in order to be successful is not covered in regular courses. His intention in this work is to share much of the information promoted in his success program books; however, within a single volume. His goal in this firstof-its-kind book is to empower and enrich readers in all walks of life with a comprehensive array of critical thinking skills, strategies, and techniques designed to give readers an edge that will help set apart from their contemporaries.

CONTENTS

FOREWORD

Many of the ideas presented in this volume were taken from parts of my most recent briefings and speeches and from my resource books developed for programs dealing with the success ethic. It was developed in response to the urgings of others to take the innovative ideas shared in my program books and put them in a single book. Their reasoning for my doing so was that a single book would be appealing to a wider audience of individuals who would rather take steps in being better on their own, instead of in a group setting.

In constructing this volume, my aim has been to introduce a number of topics that I believe are essential for success-oriented people to have in their arsenals of knowledge, and to make short work of putting the subject material into forms that an be adapted for one's personal use. The vast majority of the topics are presented as super tips. I call them *super* because I see a super tip as a loaded message with more than one face, and because it allows you to use all of the message, or just the part seen as meaningful in giving you an edge on your fellows in the arena of success.

Contained within the first eleven chapters are over 40 tips, strategies, formats, and techniques designed to strengthen and build up one's skills and critical thinking abilities. The final chapter is devoted to amalgamating 30 tips that may be seen as fail-safe stratagems. These were designed to cover broad landscape on being better, winning friends, and influencing people. My intention throughout has been to present each of the topics addressed in a manner that will capture and hold your interest while causing you to feel self-improvements as you progress through the book.

Holland Eldridge Bynam
Pearland, Texas
February, 2012

PREFACE

This book is about building "A Better You" for both yourself and your children. The Book -- All You Need To Know suggests rightly that it contains information and special tips that serve as keys to an individual's ability to achieve self-improvement. The tips, formats, and strategies presented are the result of my over 50 years of observing what works best in training others to be improved. My interest in helping others improve themselves started while a young lieutenant assigned to prepare U.S. Army military personnel for what in my opinion is the greatest challenge of all— confronting the enemy in armed combat where only the best man walks away the victor. Later, after noticing the rather dismal results from efforts employed in the education field to increase student achievement, I introduced new concepts that others believed were important in reforming the educational landscape and changing the way of motivating students to be more successful. This book combines much of what I have gleaned from two long careers about setting oneself apart so that those inclined to better themselves can begin doing so at page 1.

My overall purpose is to provide readers with a variety of advantage-producing outlooks and skills that will set them apart from their fellows. While part of my reasoning for doing so includes the need to provide others with success strategies not covered elsewhere; to assist others with ideas that promote critical thinking, with problem-solving devices for dealing with issues that may seem complex; the major reason is to provide them with the armament to overcome certain aspects of fear that I, myself, faced during my first career. Back then in thinking that certain information was being held back or denied me in many cases, and that my peers would overtake me in other cases, I used fear as a motivator to practice and learn new and improved techniques. In looking back, however, I see that the fear I felt produced positive results.

Although I now refer to this type of fear as "Righteous Fear" in my success programs, I believe it to be the driving force for Tiger Woods—one of the world's greatest athletes; for Bill Gates—one of the world's richest men; and for all who strive to set themselves apart. With this reasoning it is not difficult to understand why many professionals look to special coaches, mentors, or advisors to tip them off regarding specifics that are outside the general stream of knowledge. Nor is it difficult to see why people like Tiger Woods and Bill Gates who obviously intend to perfect their crafts, help others, and be effective organizationally, are open to new ideas that will enlarge their outlooks, skill sets, and their survival arsenals.

While those who are occupy top positions in the competitive arena close out all stops in dealing with such righteous fears, I see it is a call for all who wish to be regarded as high individual achievers to arm themselves with advantage-producing information. This book is intended to meet this call while making short work for these others in internalizing the topics presented herein. It should be noted that the expositions within the chapters are not only intended to drive home the points being developed, but to serve as guides that will allow readers to more readily adapt many of the stratagems for immediate use. I believe that if readers of the book are encouraged to adopt the many views presented, or to self-mentor themselves in developing similar methodologies for their personal use, they cannot help but have an edge on their fellows, be more all-around, and be much better prepared to meet the challenges of this century.

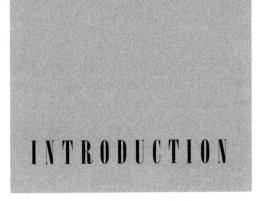

INTRODUCTION

Turning tips into strategies for setting oneself apart from others

"I wish I knew then what I know now" is an expression often heard by persons when looking back over their lives at scenes that would have had more successful outcomes if they had been better armed with information they now have in dealing with the situation being recalled. When looking back to past years, I find myself thinking of how much better my relationships and performances would have been if I knew then what I have finally come to know.

The professors and classmates on the college scene who predicted that I would have a great future, were right; however, they could not have dreamed that I was not as ready as I should have been for the challenges to be faced at the beginning of my first career. While no one is to blame for my shortcomings back then, it is a fact that a great deal of what we need to know about ourselves, about others, and about dealing successfully with a number of ordinary life challenges is not covered in schools and other training programs. This fact is the reason for my decision to share some things, by way of tips, that will help others help themselves in becoming more knowledgeable and powerful.

We can hardly escape the notion that the powerful and the great people become so due to their own hard work, but it is a certainty that most those who have achieved greatness will give credit to another who said or wrote something that was the critical spark that ignited a flame in them to set themselves apart from their fellows. In most cases the spark referred to came in the light of a unique tip that caused them to see their objectives more clearly, and aroused in them a deep desire to expand their knowledge and skills.

While being very good is the desired nature of most individuals, the act of encouraging others to become better is not easily done. This is mainly because the driving force for being better has less do with the urgings or the tips of others, and more to do with how such urgings and tips are received, internalized, and adopted as useful keepsakes for dealing with future issues. The problem is that most people see themselves as very desirable as they stand; and when feeling they are being urged by others to change in any way, they, seeing this as a challenge to their uniqueness, remain steadfast. They change only after acknowledging that they are limited in some way, and decide to take steps in order to make their limitations less severe.

Although many successful outcomes occur due to tips received on an issue of concern, in many instances where failures occur because the tip given was not internalized as a strategy for personal use, the problem may be traced to actions on the part of the tip giver. The following little story depicting a real life experience of mine is intended to highlight such a situation. It's purpose is to emphasize that tips developed for personal and organizational improvement programs should be based on a philosophy of wholeness, wherein knowledge of how overall excellence is attained is the first objective.

As a department head in preparing my organization consisting of 25 separate Junior ROTC units for a major inspection, I elected to e-mail each of the instructor leaders at the schools a set of 15 tips that were developed to insure that each of their units made an outstanding score on the multi-faceted evaluation. These tips were specific to each major area to be graded, and were carefully designed to cover key points for: meeting the inspectors upon arrival; conducting the unit's formal briefing, to include points to be highlighted and the best way to present these points; and for standardizing the responses expected of the unit's members when asked questions pertinent their roles and responsibilities. During an inspection rehearsal, after finding that one unit leader had not made hard copies of the tips provided, and had not included them in his preparations to deal with inspection specifics, I called him to task.

This unit leader, after acknowledging his oversight, assured me that I could depend upon him to always do his best. While pointing out that doing his best in this instance brought about unsatisfactory results that would have been avoided if he had utilized the tips provided, it occurred to me that my presentation method may have been faulty. Although the exact technique had worked successfully in past times, I reasoned that some individuals do not adopt tips readily probably because they generally view them as unasked for and unneeded help , and because they may see them as a challenge to their own abilities. The conclusion arrived at was that more than the mere provision of award-winning tips in written form was needed on my part, and that it would have been better to portray the ideal manner of conducting the entire inspection before providing the special tips for dealing with each part of the whole.

This led to my calling my staff and the 75 instructors to a meeting where an orientation to the inspection that included picturing the event from start to finish with not only a breakdown of the scores established for grading each part of it, but also with details showing how the tips provided would insure maximum scoring on each part. Happily, this approach resulted in each of the units being awarded special honor unit status as a result of their formal inspection performances.

When reflecting on this achievement, I came to understand that tip-giving is an art form wherein the first requirement is to ascertain that the tip giver is on the same page with all receivers. The next step is assure receivers that while the tip strategy introduced will help them in meeting their goals, additional strategies will more than likely reveal themselves during the course of utilizing it.

My revealing this story is intended to introduce the recurring theme in this book – to enrich others. The super tips within each chapter are intended to manifest themselves by directing the aim of those aspiring to be more all-around and ready to proceed with confidence in dealing successfully in the competitive world we live in. I call the tips *super* because I see a super tip as a loaded message with more than one face, whereby receivers can use all of the message, or just the part of it they see as meaningful in helping them to become more knowledgeable and more powerful. In that the idea of helping others help themselves in building a sounder philosophical base for becoming better is championed throughout the book, it is hoped that the thoughts revealed in each chapter will ultimately lead those with such a mindset to exceed their own personal improvement expectations.

CHAPTER I

ON BEING BETTER

The building blocks that will get you started!

Being a better you is much like causing a building or any other structure to become greater in excellence or higher in quality than another or others. It is, in simple terms, a process. With a building, the improvement process involves someone developing a plan for the clearing away of internal and external features that are least desirable, insuring the foundation is truly sound, and for adoring it with appealing highlights. With individuals, this process is understandably more complex. This is primarily because people with a quest for becoming more excellent must make plans to do so on their own. In this light, it is not difficult to imagine that the self-improvement plans within the folders being developed to raise one's level of excellence in a particular area will be as different among individuals as will be the personal portfolios they will establish to contain these folders.

While having mental pictures and sound structural building blocks for improvement within personal portfolios, it is important to remember that the primary focus of self-improvement programs should always be on having individuals see themselves more clearly. Next in importance is having strivers see the advantage of understanding others and interacting with these more skillfully. Both these should be a part of a personal philosophy that is grounded on being open to consider new ideas, and having a mindset to adopt for use the things drawn from said ideas that are most advantageous in dealing with their personal needs and with others in a variety of settings.

In building a philosophy of openness, the first order of work should be centered on seeking outcomes that are ideal and failsafe. This work, if based on how excellence is best attained, will lead to the adoption of a set of values that will be useful in guiding the manner in which the people, places, and things in the individuals' immediate world are treated. These values will not only serve individuals striving to better themselves, they will count immeasurably in building up their reputations as well-grounded clear thinkers, and as reliable team players.

This chapter is central to the theme of being well grounded. It is intended to set the stage for the strivers mentioned by describing certain foundational attributes that ought to be interred in the philosophy of openness that is an essential asset for those who wish to be better in dealing with themselves and others. It is thought that when these attributes are memorably implanted and made a part of the modus operandi of individuals who are committed to taking steps to become more knowledgeable, the building blocks for doing so will be soundly in place.

The seven topics within the chapter are presented mostly as one-page items. These have been selected due to their value as items that pertain to a philosophy of openness, as ideal and failsafe outcome-producers, and as suggested entries for the very first folder of individuals who are building a portfolio on being better. These topics, and the reason they were selected, are shown below:

The My and Our Rule was selected to guide one's reasoning and actions when dealing with the people, places, and things one claims ownership of.

Reputation-building Keys was selected to provide a guide list of 5 all-around tenets for individuals to build upon.

The 3 Groups of People In Our Lives and Our Concerns was selected to identify and give a brief overview of the measures one can take to present strategies that will insure sound relationships with members of each of these 3 groups that are influential in our lives.

People Within The 3 Levels Of Activity In All Organizations was selected to identify and give a brief overview of individuals found at these levels, and to offer suggestions on how to succeed within all organizations.

The Four Personality Color Groups Of People In Our Lives highlights the need to identify and understand the personality differences in those we live and work alongside, and provides tips for dealing successfully with individuals in these groups,

The Personal Checklist and Guide was developed to serve as both a model for those who see the need to develop improvement guides and as an actual checklist for successoriented persons.

The selection of Quotes To Keep And Live By was included because they are worthwhile sayings by individuals who have garnered huge reputations for their achievements in life, and because the quotes can be internalized within one's personal philosophy.

> *In that most individuals strive to do their best in dealing with tasks of all kinds, it can be assumed that all these would happily take roads to being even better if such roads were revealed to them. While the roads to being better relate to extending one's knowledge and skills, the first road to be taken is a mental one that passes through the valley of one's mind. In traveling it a person can check off the knowledge voids that should be raised to a higher level of excellence.*

The My And Our Rule

One of the most important personal rules one should embrace

In essence, this key rule refers to the expected relationship between a person and anything that the person claims ownership of by using the words "My" or "Our" in referring to it. The premise of the rule is simply that while the person claiming ownership expects something of the people, place, or thing referred to, *the objectified item* referred to expects something back from this person. A mindset for understanding this aspect goes thusly: *"The promotion of a successful relationship with another party demands thoughtful concern of the other party's expectation of you."*

As an example, if the objectified item is "my car," you expect the car to start immediately when you turn the key, to perform properly during trips, and to return you to your starting points in safety. The *car,* on the other hand, must be given credit for *having expectations* of you. It expects that you will learn of it, be observant of its safety features and fluid levels, keep its maintenance up to date, and keep it looking as close as possible to the way it looked when you first admired it. The same sort of expectation applies with respect to "my family," "my garden," "my shoes," and "my room." They apply as well with respect to things like "our teacher," "our school," "our church," "our team," "our program," etc. The point in all this is that while you always expect something of these, they should be able to expect proper action on your part in return.

Many parts of an individual's self that one puts into the MY Category fall under the purview of this rule; for example, my body, my mind, my memory, my teeth, etc. It follows that each of these parts expect some thoughtful concern on the owner's part to keep it functioning well and properly. The same goes for the places, things, and the associates, friends, and neighbors falling into the OUR Category. With the rule in mind, it is quite unnecessary to list the various things that one should do or abstain from doing regarding the people, places, and things in our lives; for when properly internalized, your responses will be so automatic that it will be difficult to avoid doing the right thing.

The most important thing to remember concerning the My and Our Rule is that *the onus is on you,* and not the people, places, or things you claim ownership of by way of using the words "my" and "our" when referring to them. In all cases, *you* are responsible for how you behave towards these; however, *you have absolutely no responsibility, or even the right,* to insist upon correcting the shortcomings or failings of your teacher, boss, parent, or others in the chain above you. In taking such a stance, you are then imposing your position on someone else without taking responsibility or having full knowledge of their jobs or their agendas. However, if you are in a leadership position where all that the group or unit does or fails to do is your responsibility, you have the obligation to take steps designed to increase the skills of the individuals involved, to improve on both their and the organization's effectiveness, and to listen to and consider their suggestions.

Reputation-Building Keys

"We want to be perceived in the same way as we perceive those we admire the most."

How an individual is seen by others depends on the estimates they have formed regarding the manner in which this person is liable to conduct himself when no one else is looking. These estimates are formed on the basis of: 1) the uniqueness in which he holds himself, 2) his treatment of others, and 3) how he will most likely present himself in dealing with the issues of life.

Of the numerous guides for building positive reputations, the 5 keys listed below, taken from a chart developed by an unknown author, are seen as inviolable due to their being universally acceptable as simple guides for displaying the attributes upon which good reputations are built.

- Be Consistent In How You Treat Others

  Treat others like you would like to be treated. Individuals are really stepping up when they treat others like *they* would like to be treated.

- Be Consistent In Your Manners

  You get your reputation by your attitude and by the way you look, act, and express yourself. As these are the hallmarks of persons of value, it behooves those who wish to be well regarded to display these features in as positive a vein as possible.

- Play The Games Of Life Skillfully

  As there are many games in life that one must play, it behooves one to view these games from the perspectives of board game players or athletes on the field. All such players are mindful of the boundaries, the rules, the prohibitions, penalties, set plays, how to score, how to minimize being scored against, and how their roles fit in with the roles of others on their teams.

- Have Personal Rules

  While rules are for orderliness and safety, personal ones that assure both these aspects are in check reputation-wise involve: not engaging in prohibited things; being on time; carrying your share of the load; and not tolerating others who lie, cheat, or steal.

- Mind Your Business Well

  All who wish to have reputations of high regard are careful to see that their own business is managed as meticulously as possible, and they area careful to adhere to the sage advice of not passing judgments, and not involving themselves in the business of others. At the same time, those who are consistent in staying in their own lanes, in reporting completion of all jobs, and in reporting problems using the established information chain, will be seen as valuable employees.

Although you will profit internally by following to the above simple keys, remember that since others are observing you, doing so will also allow you to increase your stature and acceptance among these, enhance your opportunities for success, and establish an outstanding reputation.

The 3 Groups Of People In Our Lives And Our Concerns

Know your role in dealing with people groups in order to make yourself unique

While one of the most important requirements for being better is to understand that there will always be 3 groups of the people in our lives no matter how powerful or rich or poor we may become, it is imperative that we have strategies for dealing with these, and for making our relationships with these folk wholesome and successful. The short discussions in this section are intended to identify and highlight the basic ideals for interacting with persons within these groups. While the concerns one has for people in each of these groups are embodied in the responses to Questions 1 and 2 below, it behooves wise individuals interested in building sound relationships to take pains to consider what is owed individuals in the groups identified.

The Groups of People Who Are Always in Our Lives

Those above us—Those alongside Us—Those we are responsible for

Questions:

1. Who are the people we put in these categories?
2. What are our roles in dealing properly with these individuals?

   - Those identified as being above us usually have authoritative positions. Among these are parents, grandparents, aunts, uncles, teachers, other elders, bosses, our political representatives, and even peer leaders. As these are in the category of. supporters, we should give all these the respect due their offices and our gratefulness for their efforts and contributions made on our behalf.
   - Those identified as being alongside us are brothers and sisters, friends, other peers, and enemies. We owe these the tenets of the Golden Rule—meaning that we should treat them like we would like to be treated. Since our reputations come from our relationship with this group, we would also do well to show ourselves as demonstrating the tenets of the Golden Rule and the Scout Laws. This means that those alongside us will hold us in high regard when we treat them as special, and are clean, trustworthy, loyal, cheerful, reverent, and are respectful of their traditions and beliefs.
   - Individuals identified as being among those we are responsible for include our children and their friends, and a variety of others whose care, protection, and well-being may become our responsibility. We owe all those in this group an upright character, understanding, patience, kindness, forgiveness, and additional chances. To some in this group we also owe training, discipline, and leadership.

5

People Within The 3 Levels Of Activity In All Organizations

> *Knowing where you fit in and the role you are expected to play is the first identifying feature of the high achiever.*

One can be certain that there are 3 levels of activity in all organizations, and just as certain that when one takes care to understand where he or she fits in at a specific level within an organization, and commits to meeting the expectations of that level, nothing can stop that person from being successful within it.

> *Workers at the topmost positions: (Leadership, Senior Management, etc.)*
> *Workers at the level above the base: (Unit Leaders, Staff*
> *Workers, Committee Members) Workers at the base level: (Team Leaders, Primary Workers)*

Concerns: we are concerned about three major things:

a. What is provided by those located within the three organizational levels.
b. How to meet our responsibilities when playing roles at each level of work.
c. How we can contribute to both our own and to an organization's success.

Because most individuals are involved at two or more levels in most organizational constructs, it behooves them to have a precise idea of the primary workings within each of these levels. The following is intended to describe the workings thereof:

The Upper Level

This level consists of the governing authority that presides over the major business interests of an organization. This body is usually organized in a formal manner with a leader or chairman at its head. While the members may be strangers to the base organizations being controlled and to workplace procedures, they are selected on the basis of their reputations, personal and business experience, and their special skills. At this level individuals are utilized in a variety of ways in efforts to achieve organizational success. As examples: 1) they develop strategic goals and objectives, institutional policies, raise funds, and establish budgets to insure meeting the financial objectives of the organization are met; 2) they provide administrative, logistical, training, and operational support, and 3) they maintain an active communications system for receiving reports and passing on information. While doing so, they keep abreast of the administrative and operational status of subordinate organizations, as well as the effectiveness of the entire scope of organizational leadership by way of periodic formal inspections.

When there is no superior organization to this body, the members are responsible for playing their individual and group roles that deal largely with planning and coordinating operations. In most cases these members are evaluated on the successful performances of the organization; however, when the body consists of leaders and staff members of a military style organization having a governing body over it, the members are evaluated in accordance with an existing appraisal system. In such a case, each member is appraised as if he or she was located at the middle level.

The Middle Level

Located at this level are the head of the sub-unit and his or her assistants and staff members. The leader at this level is the all-knowing problem-solver who keeps the objectives of the upper level administrators in mind, and is not a stranger to the workplace. Assistants and staff members are responsible for advising the leader, for policy production, administration, and for providing supervision, assistance, and support to the organization's sub-units. Concerned mainly with the management and utilization of the unit's resources of time, personnel, finances, property, equipment, and supplies, they maintain records on the administrative and operational status of all sub-units under the leader's control. In addition, they establish standard operating procedures for recurring events and activities, and conduct periodic informal check-ups in order to insure that both their and their sub-units meet or exceed the administrative and operational performance standards that will be evaluated by the higher authority.

While the primary leader of this organization is evaluated by the leader in the upper level having direct governance, all others are evaluated by either the primary leader or by the staff leader having supervisory authority over them. To be highly valued at this level, individuals take pains to conduct middle level business as participating team members, while displaying the attributes of base level leaders and workers with respect to the utilization of the tools and equipment items that are essential in carrying out their duties.

The Base Level

Teams and workers within sub-organizations are located at this level. Individuals located at this level are responsible for knowing their jobs, obeying all directives, adhering to organizational policy, and performing all tasks assigned to the best of their ability. High achievers at this level are able to operate responsibly in a team-working environment while displaying mastery in utilizing the tools and equipment items that are essential in completing their duties. Not only must these work to become skilled performers in utilizing assigned equipment, but also for trouble-shooting equipment disorders, and caring for equipment items.

While team leaders at the base level are evaluated by their middle level leader, they are required to appraise the performances of their subordinates. Team leaders of high value take pains to understand the criteria established for each position within their organizations, and are careful to develop standard procedures for recurring events, as well as for special procedures that are subject to informal and formal evaluations.

When an individual is aware of where he fits in at a specific level of organizational activity, and is committed to meeting all expectations of the role he is playing, he will not only be in line for advancement, his stature, influence, and reputation within the organization will be increased.

The Four Personality Color Groups Of People In Our Lives

A Powerful Key To Understanding and Dealing With Others

Interestingly enough, the Army was one of the first major organizations to promote the idea that there are four basic personality colors of people in our midst. As the idea is sound, and since in every group it is almost a certainty to find each of the four personality colors in its membership, it is important to know of them. Also, it behooves individuals who wish to build strong social and occupational relationships to understand that each of these different, but powerful personalities that are observable in individuals of all ages and stations in life.

The 4 personality colors, along with our primary concerns and their basic descriptions are shown below:

<u>Brown</u>: "The Builder," is a straightforward, no-nonsense leader type.
<u>Green</u>: "The Planner," is interested in being informed and in helping others.
<u>Blue</u>: "The Relater," is interested in how they and others are treated.
<u>Red</u>: "The Adventurer," is a risk taker who prefers exciting things.

Our Primary Concerns

The first concern is being able to recognize the innate personality colors among those around us. Next, we need to understand their personality needs and how to deal successfully with these individuals in these categories in both social and leadership situations. In that each color category requires a different strategy, one set must be adapted for dealing with each category in one-on-one situations, and a separate set must be adapted for dealing with groups containing all four personality colors.

These categories are more generally described below:

<u>The BROWN Personality:</u>
  Likes to lead and to direct others—Is a no-nonsense person—Likes to get on with the job—Is mission oriented.

<u>The GREEN Personality:</u>
  Likes to solve problems – Is a creative and strategic thinker—Likes to plan actions thoroughly—Likes to involve others in reviewing ideas—Is a proactive performer.

<u>The BLUE Personality:</u>
  Is people-oriented—Likes for all to be courteous—Is interested in fairness—Is concerned about being a good host—Likes to see folk being both congratulated and rewarded for their work.

The RED Personality:

Likes fast moving activities—Is easily bored, and sometimes forgetful—Has bright ideas—Likes fun things—Is rarely worried about things.

The Advantage of Knowing About Color Personalities

Individuals who understand the different likes and dislikes of those in each color category has the advantage of knowing how to estimate their actions and reactions, and how to use their innate qualities singly, as well as in consort, in furthering group efforts. It is essential to remember, however, that each color category is uniquely similar in:

- Having a primary disposition (what they like to do).

- Having a prevailing attitude and concern (what turns them on, what turns them off, and their orientations towards themselves and others).

Bringing The 4 Color Personality Categories Into Play

Although knowledge of the basic inclinations of each color personality category and how they can be used to your advantage is a valuable key to becoming a better you, it should be understood that neither category is deemed to be superior to either of the others. In that the primary outlooks of these personality types seldom change, it is necessary for you to factor in each color category's primary dispositions and the prevailing attitudes and concerns identified with these categories when planning to conduct activities in group settings of all kinds. While the basic drives and concerns of each category are matters to be kept in mind due to their impact on your success, be mindful also that serious leaders bring their understanding of *the "stop" an*d *"go"* buttons for each of the color categories into play in order to successfully manage an organization's most important resource—its personnel.

When wishing to signal that you value the sensibilities of others, you should be careful to take special pains to insure that you push the positive *"go"* buttons—those that equate to the preferences of the color personalities, while avoiding the *"stop"* buttons—those that may be gleaned from understanding what is *not preferred* by those individuals whose color personalities are being recognized. As a leader, when conducting activities in the social and business arenas where the color personalities are not easily recognizable, you should be aware that all four color personalities are present, and take steps by way of positive planning to insure that the dispositions and the prevailing attitudes of each category are brought into play.

The following is intended as food for thought for those who wish to insure each personality color category is brought into play during daily interaction with others and in their planning to conduct meetings of a dynamic nature. While such thinking brings the preferences of the collective group into play, it is easy to see that it serves to assist leaders in developing formats that are not only functional, but that are also keyed to causing meetings and social engagements to be satisfying experiences for all involved.

- **Brown** personality folk, because they are serious and business-like performers, their concerns should be factored into planning for all formal meetings. Therefore, it is incumbent on those who wish to make a positive impression while satisfying those having this personality color, to make sure that meetings are business-like. They should also insure that the task(s) are identified and dealt with in a straight-forward manner.

9

- **Green** personality individuals like structure. Therefore, in order to impress, satisfy, and employ individuals with this color personality gainfully, you should insure that an agenda is on hand and followed. You should also insure that as much information as possible concerning the major issues to be resolved are identified, so that the problem-solving skills of those in this color personality category can be brought into play.

- **Blue** personality people are concerned with recognition issues, and with a sense of prevailing niceness. Therefore, you should look for opportunities to thank everybody for being present and on time, and to give applause to those whose efforts have contributed to organizational success.

- **Red** personalities like action, speed, fun, and excitement. Therefore, you should make sure that the meetings move along in accordance with the agenda, and that there is room for lightheartedness. In long meetings, you must plan for timely breaks wherein refreshments or entertaining music are on hand to help insure the atmosphere is a relaxed one.

What category fits your personality? Take a few minutes and identify your friends and associates' personality colors, and then consider how you would change your interactions with them in order to have greater influence and a stronger personal relationship with them.

Personal Checklist And Guide

Being a better you requires a realistic self-assessment and a very strong determination to rise above your present state.

As a first step in developing a personal checklist and guide, one should be willing to divest himself or herself of former conditionings that have little or no value. These usually promote an untrue picture of reality, and a warm, but false feeling that there will be no need to improve oneself in any way. Examples of statements derived conditionings that individuals should divest themselves of are: *"I'm OK as I am"*; "I've been there and done that" ; and "I don't need the help of anyone." The second and most important step that one must take is to compile a list of ideals for rising above one's present condition.

An individual's personal improvement list of goals that may be written in the form of goals or in the form of questions that are the embodiment of their goals. Whatever the form, they should be reviewed periodically if for no other reason than to make oneself proud of the progress being made. Although a personal checklist may be altogether different from the one below, it is intended to serve as a self-examining guide that you should review periodically while providing a response to each question.

- Do I know myself, and am I true to this person?

- Am I a victim of false pride?

- What is the color of my personality? Do I identify and take heed of the "hot buttons' of others that I consider close associates?

- Do I treat others as I would like to be treated, and the very special folk in my life as they would like to be treated?

- Have I identified and discarded the bad habits and bad influences of the past?

- Have I identified my weaknesses and my strengths?

- Am I on track in establishing goals required to realize my dreams?

- Am I fastidious in adopting the special attributes of others I admire that can be fitted within my own personality? What are these attributes?

- Am I committed to be guided by the tenets derived from "The My and Our Rule," "The Groups of People in Our Lives and Our Concerns," "The 4 Personality Color Groups Of People in Our Lives," and by those having to do with where I fit in within various organizations?

Being able to address one or more of the questions above and make the improvements needed will score greatly in the court of personal improvement. Dealing positively with each question will free you from personal criticism.

Quotes To Keep And Live By

"Discipline yourself and others won't need to."—John Wooden

"Everyone has the will to win, but few have the will to prepare to win."—Bobby Knight

"If you don't like something, change it. If you can't change it, change your attitude." —Maya Angelou

"What you do speaks so loud that I cannot hear what you say."—Ralph Waldo Emerson

"Whether you think you can or think you can't, you're right."—Henry Ford

"The future does not get better by hope, it gets better by a plan.
And to plan for the future we need goals."—Jim Rohn

"There are no shortcuts to any place worth going."—Unknown

"Sacrifice and self-denial lie behind every success."—Vince Lombardi

"Change is a prerequisite for improvement."—Albert Einstein

"Nothing can stop the man with the right mental attitude from achieving his goal;
nothing on earth can help the man with the wrong mental attitude."
—W.W. Ziege

"It may not be your fault for being down, but it's got to be your
fault for not getting up." —Daniel L. Reardon

"The family is one of nature's greatest masterpieces."—George Santayana

"The dictionary is the only place success comes before work."—Unknown

"Don't just learn the tricks of the trade. Learn the trade."—James Bennis

"If you are called to be a street sweeper, sweep the streets even as Michelangelo painted, or Beethoven
composed music, or Shakespeare wrote poetry. Sweep streets so well that all the hosts of heaven and
earth will pause to say, 'here lived a great street sweeper who did his job well.'"—Martin Luther King, Jr.

"You may have the loftiest goals, the highest ideals, the noblest dreams, but
remember this, nothing works unless you do."—Nido Qubein

CHAPTER II

ON THINGS TO BE REMEMBERED

Utilizing the best of your memories

Once when speaking to a host of elderly family members of the fond memories of my interaction with each of them when young, I surprised them with a statement they seemed to think was hard to believe. When I mentioned that I retained and used a number of lessons gleaned from each of them, an aunt—my mother's sister, called me to task. She asked: *"What is it that you remember from my time with you back then?"*

I was very happy to reveal that something she said and did over forty years was etched in my mind. This was when I had tried and failed to pick a hundred pounds of cotton during the last days of the summer vacation at my grandparents' farm when I was about eight years old. Telling her that I would never forget the exact words she used when noticing my disappointment in having picked only seventy-five pounds of cotton at the end of the day, her eyes lit up. These words were: *"Precious, on tomorrow, auntie will show you how to work."*

She smiled broadly when I told her that I remembered her congratulatory words the next day when I was able to pick 99 pounds using the technique she gave me, but tears of joy formed in her eyes when I made my next statement. It went:

"Your help in really teaching me how to work ranks among the top of all the lessons I have learned from my family members. You should know that since that time the many laurels of recognition I have won were largely due to basing my efforts in dealing with difficult problems on the most efficient and economical way to tackle them."

With that little story as a backdrop, I have selected two pieces for this chapter. Although both refer to earlier times, I believe that success-oriented persons will agree that remembering the tenets that can be derived from them will relate to their quest to improve themselves.

The first of these, entitled *The Kindergarten Experience*, it is about one of our earliest formal learning experiences and its importance as a guideline for living wholesomely. It stems from my being entranced enough to look into a book by Robert Fulghum, the American minister and author, entitled *"All I Really Need to Know, I Learned in Kindergarten."*

In his book of essays Mr. Fulghum listed 16 simplistic things he had learned, such as "wash your hands," "don't hit others," and "put things back." Although thinking such a position had merit, I decided to make a short study to determine if a deeper meaning could be derived from the kindergarten experience. As my findings seemed to justify the assumption that this experience had a greater value than most people realized, I have not failed to promote it as an important piece of one's personal history to be placed in one's memory bank. The following notes from this study have been developed in order to outline the lessons that I feel are automatically derived from this early experience.

The Kindergarten Experience

While it is not touted as such, the kindergarten program ranks first in importance of all formal training programs. My belief is that this early experience—which involves the building up of home, schooling, and life skills – serves to set the stage for dealing wholesomely with events and occurrences taking place throughout one's life.

In my opinion, there are at least seven major life skill principles that can be derived from the earliest of school experience that continue to be important guides individuals of all ages and stations in life. While these are listed as tenets on the chart below, the practical views that follow are intended to lend clarity concerning each and amplify their implications for present-day concerns.

7 Tenets Derived From The Kindergarten Experience

1. Ask for the help of others when we are unable to do certain things on our own.
2. Establish standard operating procedures for those things that occur on a daily or periodic basis in order to conserve on time and energy.
3. Understand that rules are made for safety and orderliness, and that we should take pains to not break them..
4. Understand that it is not proper to engage in things that are prohibited.
5. Understand that people should strive to be expert in the tools used in their trade.
6. Understand that all are appraised and evaluated on their personal qualities and on their job performances.
7. Set aside special periods for dealing with daily issues and that contribute to our health and well being.

Practical Views of The Kindergarten Tenets

The Need Of Others: Back then, a kid could not do many things for himself, to include: bathing, dressing, fixing food items, or even catch a bus; even now, there are things that one is unable to do without help. It is necessary therefore, to not only establish alliances, and not only to ask for the help of others with those things we are unable to do for ourselves, but to be considerate of those who help us.

Standardizing Things: Back then, in school there were seating plans and other procedures to be followed daily to include: lining-up for movement; walking on the right hand side of the hallway, and raising hands to speak. Now we know that the best thing one can do is to establish a standard procedure for doing those things that recur on a daily or periodic basis.

Rules: Back then, there were several to follow, such as: raising hands for permission to speak or be excused; putting things back where they belong; and using titles like Miss, Missus, Mister, and perhaps, Reverend, when addressing teachers, the dean, and the principal. Now we know that there is safety in following protocol; t that rules are made to establish order and guide proper conduct; and that the breaking of rules tends to diminish our reputations, and lead to penalties of one kind or another. Driving rules, for example, promote safety and order; however, not following them may lead to negative consequences. Among these are: fines, confinement, property damage, injury, and loss of life.

Prohibitions: Back then, a number of things was prohibited, among them were no gum chewing, no fighting, no tattling, no cheating, and no lying. Even making excuses was frowned on. We know now we are better off when we do not engage in prohibited activities, and that adhering to these same tenets are important for our reputations, and that if something is prohibited, it should not be engaged at any time or for any reason.

Using Tools Of The Trade: Back then, our tool kit consisted of a ruler, protractor, colors, pencils, and eraser. Now, however, the tools we use at work may vary, and may include computers or other communications equipment, vehicles, or reports. We know now that if we thoroughly understand all aspects of the tools that are our stock and trade, and have skills for troubleshooting minor breakdowns and maintaining them on a cost-saving basis, we will be highly regarded in the workplace.

The Reporting Process: Back then, the evaluation process included the report card, letters to parents, and parent conferences. Even now, it is difficult to imagine that our behaviors and the manner in which we perform as being outside the reporting and evaluation arenas. It is very important, therefore, to learn the nature of the reports rendered on our interpersonal behaviors, as well as on our individual and team player performances.

Special Periods: Back then, the special periods set aside were locker-time study time, recess, playtime, singing and acting out, hand washing, and naptime. Although they are raised to a higher level of generality as we grow older, the kindergarten version of these periods constitute what is probably the most important of all lessons garnered from this experience.

Time, therefore, should be set aside for doing things one enjoys, completing things that one is responsible for, and for doing things that are important to having a healthy and fruitful life.

If it was the thing to do during the kindergarten experience, it remains so even now.
If it was not right on the kindergarten scene, it still is not right.

The Boy Scout And Girl Scout Laws – Annotated

The scout laws that were developed to guide the conduct and behavior of boys and girls, and to develop character, self-reliance, and usefulness to others have been unchanged since they were established. These are worthy to be placed in the category of things that to be remembered due to their importance in living wholesomely and in winning friends and influencing people.

The Boy Scout Law

Although the explanations provided for each of the 12 laws below are deemed to be sufficient in their own right, the annotations shown in the bold printed italics are intended to amplify the definitions provided in Boy Scout handbooks, and serve as additional guidelines for building strong reputations, and for becoming a better you.

- TRUSTWORTHY *(Reliable)* A Scout tells the truth. He keeps his promises. Honesty is part of his code of conduct. People can depend on him. ***(Refuses to agree with the wrong side)***

- LOYAL *(Faithful)* A Scout is true to his family, scout leaders, friends, school, and nation. ***(Keeps in touch with those who are special to him)***

- HELPFUL (Useful) A Scout is concerned about other people. He does things willingly for others without pay or reward. ***(Works to avoid selfish interests)***

- FRIENDLY *(Not hostile, amicable)* A Scout is a friend to all. He is a brother to other scouts. He seeks to understand others. He respects those with ideas and customs different from his own. ***(Introduces himself quickly)***

- COURTEOUS *(Gracious, considerate towards others)* A Scout is polite to everyone regardless of age or position. He knows good manners make it easier for people to get along together. ***(Refuses to say negative things of others)***

- KIND *(Tenderhearted, generous)* A Scout understands there is strength in being gentle. He treats others as he would like to be treated. He does not hurt or kill harmless things without reason. ***(Is especially nice to elders)***

- OBEDIENT (Follows orders of those in control) A Scout follows the rules of his family, school, and troop. He obeys the laws of his community and country. If he thinks these rules and laws are unfair, he tries to have them changed in an orderly manner rather than disobey them. ***(Does what is right in the absence of orders)***

- CHEERFUL *(Pleasant, high spirited)* A Scout looks for the bright side of things. He undertakes tasks enthusiastically. He tries to make others happy. ***(Smiles when he greets others)***

- THRIFTY *(Clever manager of resources)* A Scout works to pay his way and to help others. He saves for unforeseen needs. He protects and conserves natural resources. He carefully uses time and property. ***(Avoids wasteful spending)***

- BRAVE *(Faces difficulties resolutely)* A Scout can face danger even if he is afraid. He has the courage to stand for what he thinks is right even others laugh at or threaten him.

(Refuses to follow the crowd)

- CLEAN *(Free from polluting things)* A Scout keeps his body and mind fit and healthy. He goes around with those who believe in living by these same ideals. He helps keep his home and community uncluttered. *(Is appropriately groomed at all times)*
- REVERENT *(Respects all things sacred)* A Scout is reverent toward God. He is faithful in his religious duties. He respects the beliefs of others. *(Does not use swear words)*

The Girl Scout Law

"I will do my best to be honest and fair, friendly and helpful, considerate and caring, courageous and strong, responsible for what I say and do, and to respect myself and others, respect authority, use resources wisely, make the world a better place, and be a sister to every Girl Scout"

As can be seen from the reading of the Girl Scout Law above, it, very much like the Boy Scout Law, is also a code for living wholesomely and for winning friends and influencing people. As written, the Law needs no further explanation; however, I have taken the liberty of annotating each part with additional terms in order to amplify these important guidelines.

<u>I will do my best to be</u>: *(Commit myself to be seen as …)*

- Honest and fair, *(Truthful; using good judgment)*
- Friendly and helpful, *(Cheerful; looking on the bright side, and willing to share my time and skills with deserving others who are less fortunate)*
- Considerate and caring, *(Thinking of, and keeping others in mind)*
- Courageous and strong, and *(Standing up for what is right; helping the weak)*
- Responsible for what I do, *(Refusing to do foolish things)*
- And to respect myself and others, *Keeping myself above reproach, and avoiding what would seem to be self-centered)*
- Respect authority, *(Obeying rules; giving appropriate honor to those above me)*
- Use resources wisely, *(Being careful in using time, money, equipment, and supplies)*
- Make the world a better place, *(Being a good citizen)*
- And be a sister to every Girl Scout. *(Supporting all who share my jest for life)*

CHAPTER III

ON BEHAVIOR IN A NUTSHELL

Building unwavering principles

Once when I was seated in a school lunchroom alongside two preachers and the principal, the teacher on duty was trying to get order by telling the children to *behave themselves*. One of the ministers disagreed when I mentioned that the students did not have a ready definition for the word *behave*, and that this teacher should point out exactly what she wanted the students to stop doing. The point of the minister's disagreement was that the students surely knew exactly what the teacher meant because they had been hearing this term all their lives. I retorted by stating that the term was sort of abstract, and that most folk have difficulty with abstract-like terms, even with those they hear and use a lot. When I stated that I believed that most preachers would be put on the spot if asked to define the term "love," to explain how it is done, and to give advice on how to assess whether or not the act of love was being performed properly, the second preacher interjected with: *"I must say Amen to that, my brother."*

This little story was mentioned to highlight the fact that most folk do not have ready definitions for abstract-like terms like "behave" and "love." The major point intended to be made was that not having ready definitions for terms they use daily and for activities they participate in on a regular basis, is a hindrance to their performing well. This is why a short study on behaviors covering everyday issues, guides for displaying acts that set you apart, and for dealing with those you have responsibility for is introduced in this chapter.

In thinking that one of the primary culprits in causing people to under-perform in workplace arenas and in life, my work has been oriented to addressing topics that are not covered thoroughly in either educational institutions, in self-education programs, or in training programs outside the educational community. This line of thinking has been the driving force for my efforts to help others better themselves and be more successful. I believe that folk who intend to make confident headway in the social, education, economic, and workplace arenas, are in need of ready definitions that help them in explaining the workings within their fields of interest. I feel also that success-oriented programs should be focused as much on behavior-modification as on improving fundamental skills.

My belief that this dual focus should be maintained in developmental programs and in all success-oriented training programs, stems from what I think is a failure on the part of educational systems in not putting character development on par with student achievement, and in leaving off emphasizing the behaviors expected of workers. It may be said that my success programs are focused on skill development;

however, equal emphasis is placed on the desired behaviors associated with the skills being produced. This is due to my thinking that the need or desire to improve oneself is one part of the stimulus, and knowing that one's conduct will always be open to evaluation by others is the other part. Because I am aware of the fact that one's conduct will always appraised in some way, when outlining the topics designed to assist individuals in widening their outlooks and becoming better, some aspect of how they are to behave in order to be evaluated highly is included in the narrative.

Collectively, the 3 pieces selected for this chapter are intended to add to what has gone before regarding an individual's personal behavior, and to serve as additional food for thought for those with a quest for being all-around better persons. In that the topics already covered in chapters I and II deal largely with thoughts pertaining to how individuals can take steps on a personal basis to change their outlooks in general, I believe that in providing information designed to put the topic of behavior in a nutshell, such an effort will round out the discussion.

- The first, "A Short Study on Behaviors," taken from my *All-Around Success In A Nutshell* program, is seen as pertinent to both the young and old. This study, consisting of a few pages only, is intended to condense and clarify important views on the subject. The first page lists a number of super behavior tips for everyday living. The second page identifies some of the general behaviors that worthy individuals look to display, and the third identifies several general behaviors that success-oriented individuals will do well to avoid displaying.

- The second, An Example Assessment Survey, also taken from my success program, is intended to serve as a guide and spark enthusiasm in those who supervise others to develop private documents useful in assessing their efforts as, teachers, managers, or leaders. The Example survey shown was used when I was featured as guest speaker during a parent conference to guide my talk on the behavior of parents in rearing their children. At that time it was used to serve as a useful "food for thought" item for those who were searching for more profound ways in helping to develop their children, while giving them ideas, they, themselves, would use as parents and in life in general. It is used here as an example because it can be readily modified by those with responsibilities for the development of others. As can be seen, the notes following the survey are family oriented; however, it is thought that when other such documents are developed by improvement-seeking individuals, they will do well to base them on experiences they see as having had positive impacts on their own success.

- The third, "A Composite Definition of Love," is likely to serve as a focal point for lively discussion and debate. I hold that the term 'love," in that it is essentially a behavior, it should be defined as such. I believe that since people purport to love various others and various places, and things, the act can only be shown by the manner in which one behaves towards these. Convinced that the concept *has not* been explained with sufficient clarity in books and by the clergy, the spin I offer here is meant to stimulate thought and to encourage others in agreeing with me, or arriving at their own definition of what love is. I am equally convinced that after individuals arrive at a plausible definition for themselves, they will have little trouble in being able to assess their own conduct in dealing with the people, places, and things they claim to have this affinity for. As this is last article in the chapter, it should come as no surprise that it is believed to be the most important topic in my arsenal on behaving, and the most pertinent in one's quest to become better all-around.

A Short Study On Behaviors

In that their reputations are derived from their treatment of others, and from the manner in which they show themselves as individuals of value, those who are wise will do well to establish for themselves a set of unwavering principles to abide by. I believe such principles should be formulated to cover: 1) a number of everyday issues. 2) the general behaviors that are associated with strong personal values, and 3) those behaviors that detract from building positive reputations. While a complete study covering these aspects would be extensive, I feel the three topics selected from my success program will go far in assisting others in formulating their own unwavering principles.

1. <u>Super Behavior Tips For Everyday Living</u>

<u>On Accepting Awards</u>: Do so graciously, and remember that awards usually carry with them an expectation of future conduct worthy of such an award recipient.

<u>On Acting Out</u>: Always avoid acting out. Instead of riotous laughter, it is much better to acknowledge that something is very funny or hilarious by accompanying controlled laughter, cheerfully words like *"That is hilarious."*

<u>On Backing Up A Buddy</u>: Back up buddies when they are right; avoid doing so when they are wrong. While it is OK to state the positions you agree with, stay out of the action if you don't know the facts.

<u>On Breaking Your Word</u>: It's OK only if you inform the others involved as early as possible that you will be unable to keep your word.

<u>On Copying</u>: It's only OK if you are copying the positive mannerisms of someone you admire and would like to emulate; otherwise, never copy without acknowledging the work of another.   <u>On Giving</u>: You can expect to be made to regret giving money, materials, time, and energy to undeserving individuals. Because undeserving receivers cannot help but disappoint those who give them, it is best to cause such a recipient to be deserving prior to giving him or her the boon.   <u>On Interrupting Others</u>: By avoiding the tendency to interrupt a speaker, you have an opportunity to collect your thoughts so they can be presented coherently. Instead of abruptly blurting out a question, signal that you want to be recognized and proceed with something like:

"May I ask a question, please?"

<u>On Saying Things</u>: It is a good idea to consider rephrasing the first thing that comes to your mind. Since the guideline *"There are no secrets between two people"* has been proven to have merit, it is best to say nothing that you will be embarrassed about later, and to never mouth negative words about another that could get back to this person.

<u>On Stealing</u>: It's only OK if you are stealing time away from routine things to improve your mind and body. In other cases, it is never a good idea.

<u>On Telling Others What To Do</u>: Always avoid this tendency unless your advice is asked for. In the same way as you detest receiving advice from another with no more experience than you have, the at of giving advice to another with similar life experiences is hardly ever appreciated.

2. Behaviors One Should Look To Display

People always pick the shiniest apple

While there may be other general behaviors that are associated with a person's upward movement within an organization or within society in general, wise individuals are mindful to display the following set of behaviors that are respected universally:

- Display <u>A Goal Attainment Disposition</u>—Persons having this disposition are inclined to be both people and mission-oriented, and to be habitual purveyors of winning strategies.

- Display <u>Courageousness</u>—While there are two faces for courage—physical and moral—the moral aspect is usually the one that is most prominent in reputation building. Persons are considered morally courageous when they are able to stand by convictions they have determined to be right despite the urgings of others to change their positions for ones that are more popular, but less sound.

- Display <u>Maturity</u>—While maturity is the state of being grown-up or fully developed, it is marked by a disposition to deal with problems and other issues in a serious vein, and avoid playfulness.

- Display <u>Personal Pride</u>—While personal pride is displayed by the dignity in which a person carries himself or herself, others are impressed when one 's actions denote a willingness to carry a full share of the load, and when one's efforts are seen as serious moves to cause an organization to thrive in every way.

- Display <u>Resourcefulness</u>—This behavior is shown when one is able to act effectively and imaginatively in difficult situations. While individual resourcefulness will more than likely be rewarded in an organizational setting, it is most valuable when individuals involve their team members in the thought process, and also when they encourage team members to help in developing procedures emanating from group ideas for solving problematic situations.

- Display <u>Self-Worthiness</u>—Self worthiness is displayed by maintaining a quality about oneself that equates to putting others first, and being useful, admirable, and honorable.

- Display <u>The Need To Better Oneself</u>—This need is shown as a result of a realistic self assessment wherein it becomes obvious that one must improve his knowledge and skills in order to be more successful in dealing with the issues of life. Individuals who display a willingness to study and to seek advice regarding key issues of concern, are always held in high regard.

- Display <u>The Need To Make A Difference</u>—This need is shown as a result of an assessment of one's immediate environment, and is evidenced by an obvious commitment to help others be better performers, and by actions taken to increase one's own as well as his organization's effectiveness.

3. <u>Behaviors One Should Avoid Displaying</u>

The following list of general behaviors are among the major ones that are seen as being universally unacceptable. In that they detract from building highly regarded reputations, and because they tend to beset opportunities for advancement within an organizational construct, success-oriented individuals will do well to avoid displaying any of these behaviors at all times:

- <u>Being Callous</u>. Callous folk are emotionally hardened, and are unable to put themselves in another's place.

- <u>Being Disrespectful</u>. Disrespectful folk are those who by their words, deeds, and attitudes, demonstrate a lack of regard for others.

- <u>Being Fearful of Success</u>. This tendency is demonstrated by those who fear they have inadequate skills to move to a higher position, or that they will lose the respect of peer group personnel they will seem to outshine.

- <u>Being Intolerant of Others</u>. Intolerant folk are those who cannot accept the different opinions and beliefs held by others.

- <u>Being Un-teachable</u>. This tendency is demonstrated by folk who have no faculty for learning, those who have hardened themselves against learning in general, and those who have set themselves to be resentful of others who seem determined to help them be more successful.

- <u>Displaying Boredom</u>. While being bored is an emotion resulting from something being dull, the outward display of this emotion seems to signal that individuals will not have the mental energy to suppress the need for meaningless excitement, nor the ability to discern the value of an idea that may be presented in a rather dull manner.

- <u>Having False Pride</u>. False pride is a foolish self-assessment of strengths that are not really present in the person. Such persons do not see the need for training and practice in order to acquire the strengths they claim for themselves.

- <u>Showing Lack of Pride</u>. This behavior is evident when persons do not think enough of themselves to endure discomforting measures, even when these will be essential in changing their present conditions for the better. In a group setting, this behavior is demonstrated when some individuals follow negative-minded others who tend to reject advice calling for social, educational, and attitudinal changes that when made will assure them a better future.

An Example Assessment Survey

The scope of this survey, while intentionally comprehensive, was not meant to evaluate current home situations, or to infer that the questions pertain to a malady that besets today's family construct. Nevertheless, it is noteworthy to mention that the vast majority of the parents taking part in the original survey admitted to having overlooked at least one-half of the items listed.

	Yes	No
1. Does your family eat together more than once each week?	___	___
2. Does your child have a special seat at the table during meals?	___	___
3. Is a specific place set-aside for your child to study?	___	___
4. Is the place set aside for study well lighted?	___	___
5. Is there a specified "study time period" designated for your child?	___	___
6. Is your child's homework checked by a grownup?		
7. Do you set aside quality time to discuss family matters with your child and to see if the child has any problems?	___	___
8. Do you have an open calendar in your home for scheduling activities that involve family members?	___	___
9. Are children in your household assigned designated chores?	___	___
10. Is the lifetime goal your child has selected one that he/she will be able to reach?	___	___
11. Have you selected at least one activity for your child to assist him/her to be a well rounded person?	___	___
12. Are rewards/penalties in place in your home concerning the accomplishment of short-term goals?	___	___
13. Do you make periodic visits to speak with your child's teachers?	___	___
14. Do you encourage your child to save money?	___	___
15. Do you encourage your child to write letters to or to call grandparents and other supporters?	___	___

Notes Pertinent to The Parental Assessment Survey

Reference Item 1: (The Family's Eating Together)

A perfect time to bond with and find out how your child is doing academically, socially, and otherwise, is while dining together. This time together also allows the child to know more about his her parents and their concerns. Were it not for this period in my life, my stepfather would not have noticed that my brother and I needed training in dining room social graces, and in handling eating utensils. His teachings thereafter helped us become expert at setting the table and handling knife, fork, and spoon. When we became teenagers, eating together was a time for sharing information and learning how we could have handled a problematic situation more delicately from our parents. It did not take long to figure out that they were more experienced in just about everything we were involved in at the time.

Reference Item 4: (A Place Set Aside To Study)

Since there were only two siblings in our home, a place for each to study was not a major problem even though our house was not expansive. Because we had to complete our school assignments before playing, sometimes chores and lengthy school requirements meant no play at all that day; especially when additional school work was required after dinner. Making special times for play was not a premium at our home because our parents knew that students played during the gym period at school, and because they allowed us to be members of school athletic teams. In addition, because the two of us were interested in playing musical instruments, we were encouraged to view practicing our music lessons as play periods.

Reference Item 7: (Parent-child Discussions)

When my brother and I speak of these times, we tend to agree that we learned more about dealing with family life and being successful in general while being with our parents in the evenings after dinner. The dining table was the spot for reviewing planned activities wherein the entire family was to be together. We discussed many things while there, including scheduled school activities, parental support that would be required for these activities, and scheduled visits to be made where all family members were to be together. This is also where we were reminded of promises made, and of "thank you notes" that were due some supporter.

Reference Item 8: (Use Of The Open Calendar)

Lately, when visiting my brother, I noticed that he, too, keeps a calendar much like that used years before by our parents to remind him of commitments,. Back then, however, church, visits, special school events, and special chores, were the first entries put on this calendar by one of our parents. When the fun things the boys wanted to do did not conflict with the initial entries, they were entered upon approval. At present, my brother uses one at work during his team orientations to inform its members of the status of goals; and to remind them of the time something is expected of them, and of the dates they could expect the support of others.

Reference Item 10: (The Child's Lifetime Goal Selection)

Hopefully, counseling students on their lifetime goals has been improved on since my early days when I stated my goal of being a doctor was applauded by my teachers. Unfortunately, none of them told me that the key to medical training was chemistry, and the key to chemistry was algebra. Had I been so advised, I would have been more fastidious in studying math, taken chemistry classes during my high school years, and would have had an easier time in college. It follows that a parent can help a child determine if a certain lifetime goal is appropriate by assisting him in determining what learning is required in pursuit of it, and what essential work will be necessary in reaching such a goal.

A Composite Definition Of Love

What is love, and what is required of lovers?

My interest in developing practical definitions for terms that seemed abstract on the surface began when I realized the advantage of having a ready response for describing the basic requirements of the fields of work I was involved in, and a ready response for describing the universal expectations of workers in these fields. And while I have encouraged managers, leaders, coordinators, and others to follow my lead in developing practical definitions for their lines of work, I stumbled up on a practical definition for the abstract-like term *"love"* during my tenure as a Sunday School teacher at my church. Although I had not given thought to developing a ready response for describing the act of love, I surprised myself by having the nerve to lecture a pastor I respected highly, and in doing so learned a lesson that caused me to be a better me.

During a bible teaching session, since the pastor mentioned the aspect of loving one another several times during his discourse, I asked if he would tell what love is, how to teach it to others, and how to tell if we were doing it correctly? He agreed to do so, and began with explaining both brotherly and agape love—that which gives and sacrifices and expects nothing back in return. Although I was not really surprised, he then went off into the blue, so to speak, and ended by saying," God is love, and that since God was too big to explain, the concept of love could never be fully explained."

I followed him into his office and asked why would he leave us in a lurch with such a nebulous response? "After all," I said, "you have been teaching that the commandment made by Jesus concerning the act of love served to replace the Ten Commandments. And if the commandments were established to guard against bad behavior, I believe we have part of he answer." I continued by saying, "In that the Master told his disciples to love one another as He had loved them, and since we know that what he did was to not only take care showing concern for their feelings, but also to teach, lead, and bless them, it seems that we can say without reservation that the concept of love is based on proper behavior."

In thanking him for abiding me in this instance, I asked the pastor to please give this some thought, and then give us a sermon later extolling the fact that love can be simply defined as proper behavior; that it can be taught using the tents of proper behavior as a guide; and that when we can determine that we have said or done something to another that we, ourselves, would not have appreciated if the same was done to us, we know that we are violating the code."

While this little story is intended to identify the biblical components for defining love, if we agree that all of what we signal by our attitudes, and all of what we say and do are categorized as behaviors, we must also agree that love, itself, is a behavior; and that behaving properly toward a person, place, or thing is the sole requirement in loving these.

"Loving and having passionate feelings must be put in two different categories. Passion, is an emotion that can even be displayed in anger or in hatefulness. Love, on the other hand, has all to do with behaving properly."

CHAPTER IV

ON THE FOUNDATIONAL ASPECTS OF IMPROVEMENT

Reading, Writing, and 'Rithmetic,

If one were to say that a person just met was intelligent, it would more than likely be that that person seemed to project himself as one who used his ears more than his mouth, as an alert and quick-witted responder, as well-read, and as one who seemed to have the requisite skills for managing his affairs effectively. Although such an assessment would not normally be argued against, I am convinced that there are skills for making these projections a reality. I take the position that while a number of strategies for intellectual improvement have been advanced, most of these have not categorized or presented as intelligence-building within the curricula frameworks of our schools and universities.

Among the strategies referred to in a number of articles on improvement are:

- work on your vocabulary,
- read good books,
- watch the news,
- cultivate an interest in current events,
- listen carefully to the opinions of others,
- exercise your mind, and
- visit new places.

While agreeing that this listing is important, I maintain that if individuals are oriented to becoming more intelligent, the focus should be a collective one that includes the acquisition and retention of knowledge and skills that can help them in coping with the strategies just listed. These folk need to be build up skills for memorizing and recalling critical issues and facts, and for employing language that signifies they have sound reasoning, observation, and problem solving abilities.

It should come as no surprise that I believe the aspect of intelligence production can be boiled down in simple terms, and that the discussion should start with definitions for both knowledge and intelligence. Since knowledge is defined as *"understanding gained through study and experience,"* and since intelligence is *"the capacity to acquire and apply knowledge,"* it is safe to say that four pillars—*Speaking, Reading,*

Writing, and '*Rithmetic*—constitute not only the bedrock of education, but also the basis on which one's intelligence stands. It follows that all who are interested in cultivating and improving upon skills pertaining to these four pillars should be open to tips centered on practical applications for employing each of these foundational acts more effectively.

Interestingly enough, the order in which the pillars are listed above is the natural order that they are introduced in life and developed within the education process. Although the first, speaking, is the most obvious sign of one's intelligence, I have elected to devote a separate chapter, Chapter X, to the art of speaking well.

This chapter, concerned with the basic academic skills essential to the remaining pillars known widely as the "3 R's," is divided in three parts. Although several entries have been selected for each of these parts, the 3 parts are generally described below:

- Part 1 is dedicated to the reading realm. The five entries selected for this part are intended to motivate and assist you in comprehending written material, and to embolden you in seeking out and retaining information.

- Part 2 consists of nine topic entries centered on the art of writing. This part is more extensively developed because of the notion that information pertinent to the art of thinking well is more easily brought out in the writing realm, and because individuals committed to being more skillful in this realm cannot help but benefit from the collective information introduced.

- Part 3, entitled *Rithmetic*, does not concern itself with mathematics per se. The 4 topics introduced are intended to show that individuals can increase their chances for being successful by utilizing concepts that add to their abilities in reaching goals, conserving their efforts, dividing their time more wisely, and in eliminating potential problems that occur in everyday life.

PART 1

READING

Although reading is the cornerstone for the act of study; the term, "reading well," is too often used loosely. Even a child is said to be able to read when it can utter or render aloud words it recognizes; however, being able to grasp the meaning of written or printed characters, words, or sentences must be cultivated if one is to be categorized as an able reader. Because the vast majority of this world's knowledge is locked away in books or in computer memory, individuals desiring to widen their outlooks and abilities will find that their quest for becoming more knowledgeable is directly related to their zeal for becoming more skillful information seekers when using these tools.

The four topics selected for this part of the chapter are seen as bridges for gaining information, grasping ideas more quickly, and for leaping a number of hurdles encountered along the journey to success. Collectively, these are intended to increase your reading and comprehension skills, motivate you to build upon these skills, and open the door to where a world of information may be found for your enlightenment, joy, and usefulness.

- "The Really Reading Concept" was first developed to help high school students understand more clearly how an author develops his ideas, and to introduce a mechanism that will help them in grasping ideas and in presenting their own ideas with firmness. It is included here because educators and professionals who were given briefings on the concept were of one accord. All indicated that they, themselves, benefited from this concept, and that it should be shred with audiences of all kinds.

- The entry, Comprehension Tips For Readers, gives tips on key methods for grasping what an author's intends to introduce, and on placing this information in a memory context.

- The entry, <u>Problems Overcome By Great People</u>, covers short vignettes on Presidents Lincoln and Eisenhower, and on General Powell and Malcolm X. The purpose of these vignettes is show how individuals brought up in different periods and under entirely different circumstances, were able to gain and use their knowledge derived from extensive reading to elevate themselves, meet goals, and impact others.

- <u>The Reference Library Advantage</u> gives entry points to the many helpful things that can be found in this comprehensive volume containing a wide variety of useful information. It points also to the fact that having such a volume as a part of one's personal library is a helpful tool in making short work of learning about a number of complex issues.

" The Really Reading Concept"

Improvement by way of reviewing basic skills largely forgotten

The "Really Reading Concept" was developed to dynamically connect authors with readers in order to improve students' skill in dealing with basic information. When first presented to my staff and the 75 instructors I supervised, I visited the 25 high school Junior ROTC programs I had the honor of directing. When there, I had the pleasure of sharing the concept with the cadet officers in the junior and senior classes. I always began by asking the groups of students if they could read well?

I'm sure you can imagine the responses these honor students gave me, but I informed my staff recommended that if I shared my new concept with the students their reading skills would not only improve, their comprehension, writing, and speaking skills would be improved. I always got their full attention by announcing that my "Really Reading Concept" would help in strengthening their test-preparation skills, and that it took only about 6 minutes to explain.

I began by telling them that one-half of the strategy was imbedded in 4 questions that I would provide answers for in the interest of time.

The questions were as follows:

1. Why do authors write books and periodicals?
2. What is the purpose of a sentence?
3. What is the purpose of a paragraph?
4. What types of sentences do we find in paragraphs, and what purposes do they serve?

My responses to the questions were these:

- Authors write books and articles to share their ideas with readers.

- The purpose of a sentence is *to express a complete thought.*

- The purpose of a paragraph is *to develop one idea.*

- The types of sentences that are contained within the paragraph are *topic, supporting, and concluding sentences,* wherein:

  a. Topic sentences *always express the main idea.*

b. Supporting sentences are sentences within the paragraph that always *support the topic sentence.* They do so by: *providing facts, details, explanations, examples, etc.*

c. Concluding sentences are not always used; however, when employed they may function in three ways: (1) *Restating the main idea,* (2) *Summarizing information contained in the supporting sentences,* and (3) *Serving as a transition or connector to the next paragraph.*

After explaining the that keeping these facts in mind were basic to *the concept,* I told them that many authors use the introduction, supporting, and concluding technique in developing their books and chapters. Following this, I pointed out that since they seemed interested how my concept could be applied in helping with their test-preparation skills, I would explain the strategy by way of a scenario featuring a very wise student.

My remarks went as follows:

The Really Reading Concept & Test Preparation

- "Let's say the teacher announces that there will be a test on Chapter 10 in the textbook at the next meeting of the class.

  The wise student notices that there are 12 paragraphs in chapter 10."

- "By this, the student knows that the author has between 10 and 12 ideas to share in the chapter.

  The reason there may be only 10 is because the first paragraph may be the topic paragraph, and the last may be the concluding paragraph."

- "The student locates the idea in each paragraph and notes how the author develops and explains it.

  The wise student will more than likely use the dictionary to look up unfamiliar words."

- "The student then prepares a set of comprehensive test questions dealing with each idea presented on one sheet, and writes out the answers to these questions on a separate sheet.

  In this way the student develops his own test study notes, and readies himself for the true-false, fill-in, multiple-guess, or essay questions that may be asked."

At the end of our little sessions, when I asked these groups if they agreed that this concept is useful for readers, writers, speakers, and test-takers, I am happy to say that I always received a round of what I saw as grateful applause.

"Really Reading" is a superior form of reading because it causes the reader to focus on the ideas presented, on how they are supported, and on how they pertain to the general premise being developed.

Comprehension Tips For Readers

Comprehension: The act or fact of grasping the meaning, nature, or importance of; really understanding.

Although people read for a variety of reasons, including doing so to escape boredom and for pleasure, many readers have a hunger to obtain the real meat in an issue being presented. In that some of these need to grasp information clearly for dealing with examinations or work-related issues, the seven tips below are designed to assist them in understanding topics introduced in books or periodicals that may be complex.

1. Decide if your purpose is to get main ideas, facts, explanations, etc.
2. Make note of the idea developed in each paragraph, decide if the author's main idea concerns a person, place, or thing,
3. Look for facts in the supporting details.
4. When a sentence is difficult to understand, look up the meaning of new words and reread the sentence coming just before this sentence.
5. Remember the author had a definite reason for placing charts or pictures on a page. Therefore, make sure you can connect the reason for the author's doing so before leaving the page.
6. Pay special attention to *sign-post* words as indicated in italics below:

   * That mean no exception to the statement or idea already mentioned: (*all, every, always, never, etc.*)
   * That introduce more information: (*and, furthermore, moreover, etc.*)
   * That pertain to the same basic idea: (*and so, therefore, as a result, however, etc.*)
   * That indicate a change in thought: (but, although, on the contrary, despite, still, etc.)

7. Think about the ideas the author shared before going on to something new. When you expect to be evaluated on material wherein the ideas presented may be difficult to connect, it is advisable to write out a paragraph in your own words that represents the totality of what you believe the author was intending to make plain.

NOTE CONCERNING TIP #7 above: The mere reading over an author's presentation and moving on without taking time to weave the ideas introduced into a whole, is a disservice to the reader and the author. The act of thinking about the manner in which ideas have been presented before moving on to a student reading for ideas as the review of an exam that has been taken would be. While a exam review allows students to evaluate their work and get the facts right as they pertain to the items or issues guessed at, the act of thinking about what an author has shared serves a similar purpose. This is because placing the author's presentation in a memory context strengthens your ability to recall details, and is a guard against guessing incorrectly.

Problems Overcome By Great People

Being aware of how others overcame adverse circumstances sets the stage for another's betterment

Abraham Lincoln, the sixteenth President of the United States, and an avid reader, is numbered among the greatest minds produced in America. This self-taught man learned to read and write from borrowed books, and became a lawyer. Ambitious to rise in politics, he had to overcome a lot before becoming President. He failed in business twice, and had several political setbacks, including: defeats for Congressional nomination and for a Congressional seat, two defeats in seeking a Senate seat, and one defeat in a run for Vice President. Famous for *The Emancipation Proclamation*—proclaiming freedom for the slaves in 1863; and for *The Gettysburg Address*—delivered at the end of the Civil War—he is known as one of the greatest U.S. presidents.

Dwight D. Eisenhower, the thirty-fourth President of the United States, was known as "Ike." As an Army officer in the rank of major, he was *not selected* for the prestigious Command & General Staff School (C&GSC) on several occasions due to a conflict he was having with the chief of the Army's Infantry Branch who was in charge of school assignments. Without this school, Ike had no prospects to achieve very high rank; however, Brigadier General Fox Conner decided to superintend Eisenhower's education while he was assigned to the General's staff. The General introduced him to various military writers and influential thinkers via an intensive reading program, and encouraged his pupil to discuss their works and analyze their ideas and stratagems. As a result, Ike perfected his tactical and administrative techniques; and because of General Conner's influence, was allowed to attend the C&GSC. He finished with top honors and began his rise to be a 5-Star General and in command of all allied forces in the European theater during WWII. Following his retirement from the Army, he became president of a noted university before moving on to become President.

General Colin Powell is mentioned here because he was a middle-of-the-road college student, but his single-minded interest in military and studies connected with leadership and government set him apart ROTC student peers. Continuing this focus as an Army officer, he rose above his peers—some who were Rhodes Scholars—to be appointed to the very lofty positions of National Security Advisor, Chairman of The Joint Chiefs of Staff, and Secretary of State. In that his example highlights the importance of a steady aim in increasing one's knowledge within special spheres of interest, it should encourage others to aim high and to study and work to be masterful in fields for which they have a special affinity.

Malcolm X, a high school dropout at age 15, was sent to prison for burglary at age 21. While there, he copied every page in the dictionary, and built a workable vocabulary by learning the meanings of, and the power of many words he used later to influence his followers and others. After serving his prison term, he dedicated himself to building the Black Muslims, but later left that movement and founded the organization of Afro-American Unity. As founding leader, he was an outspoken speaker for human rights until his assassination at age 39. He is mentioned here because his intelligence was developed by tenaciously improving himself through reading while under the adverse condition of being incarcerated.

The Reference Library Advantage

Almost everything you need to be generally informed of is contained in one book

Because the reference library contains such a large amount of useful information, it is undoubtedly the most important single book a serious reader can have. Not only is it useful in feeding the hunger of ordinary knowledge seekers and pundits, it is advantageous to scholars, researchers, business persons, and many others who may benefit from the facts, formats, and formulas found therein. While all reference library books are divided into two major sections, *"The Dictionary Section,"* and *"The Encyclopedia Section";* the information provided is of special significance to those with limited time for research.

This piece is included in the section on reading because it is a valuable tool containing permanent information and guidelines. The topics below, displayed in *"Webster's New Reference Library for Home, School, Office,"* are typical of those covered all such reference books.

The Dictionary Section

1. How To Display The Flag
2. Useful words and phrases in 3 languages (German, French, Spanish)
3. Bible Dictionary
4. Business Dictionary
5. Biographical Dictionary of Americans Who Have Played Great Roles
6. Dictionary of Occupational Titles
7. Roget's Thesaurus

The Encyclopedia Section

1. Communications through language, including key information on:
   * *Basic Tools*: (Punctuation marks – Grammar—Spelling and vocabulary)
   * *Using the Tools*: (Effective sentences—Effective paragraphs—The total composition)
   * *Special compositions*: (The research paper—Argumentative writing—Narrative writing - Fictional narrative—Description—The book report/review—The précis—A Science project report—Mechanical details—Letters and employment—Resumes)

2. The Library—(Foreign Words and Phrases)
3. Reading Skills: (Previewing—Finding Main Ideas—Critical Reading)
4. Where to Write for Vital Records
5. The Business World: (How to make and use a family budget—How to buy a house—How to make a will—The business secretary)
6. Quick Reference World Maps
8. World History
9. American History: (American Government—The Constitution)
10. States and Countries
11. Authors and Their Works
12. Math Formulas/Equivalent Measures

13. <u>Computer Science</u>
14. <u>Biology</u>
15. <u>Physics</u>
16. <u>Four Year Colleges and Universities</u>

NOTE: The encyclopedia section contains many more topics, including: geology, astronomy, metric conversions, cooking and nutrition, and special definitions and translations found in the music, computer, and space glossaries.

PART 2

WRITING

If you can't communicate your ideas in writing, then they are lost

To write is merely to form letters, words, or symbols on a surface with an instrument such as a pen; however, the act of writing well should be a topic of concern for all who wish to express themselves more clearly on paper or its digital equivalent.

I am not shy in stating that I began to write well only after learning what good writing entails. I believe that writing well is an important skill set to have for those who wish to enhance their standing in society and in a number of professional fields, and think it is unfortunate that the topic of effective writing is generally glossed over in our schools and universities. For these reasons, this part of the chapter is dedicated to offsetting this tendency. The short extracts below, while they are intended to assist individuals who wish to become better at developing and evaluating their own written works, are also deemed worthy of being filed away as useful reference material:

In <u>Good Writers Seek To Master Punctuation Rules</u>, the punctuation marks used by writers are listed, and the rules for using them are highlighted. In that the use of punctuation marks is the first indicator of a writer's skill, individuals should endeavor to seek mastery in utilizing these governing rules.

In <u>Good Writers Seek To Master Capitalization Rules</u>, the capitalization rules are simplified in such a way that mastery of them requires an understanding of only 14 easily learned concepts.

In <u>A Simple Letter To A Child – An Example</u>, a personal letter is used to model a very simple form of outlining, and to promote the sense that the simple outlines not only serve to save time, but that they can be used also as aids for developing coherent written compositions.

In <u>Outlining Tips Worth Keeping</u>, tips on how to prepare a standard outline are highlighted.

In <u>The Formal Outline</u>, the form and the divisions of the properly developed outline are highlighted and explained.

In <u>The Formal Letter</u>, the seven parts required in all formal letters are identified; and the additional parts that may be required in business and official letters are listed, along with details explaining where and how these parts are emplaced in these letters.

In <u>Paragraph Development</u>, the 7 major ways a paragraph can be developed are named and described.

In <u>Developing Ideas—Examples Using The 7 Common Ways</u>, the same theme is utilized while demonstrating the seven ways in which ideas may be presented in a paragraph.

In <u>The Three-Paragraph Theme</u>, tips are given for dealing successfully with each paragraph.

Good Writers Seek To Master Punctuation Rules

Editors and others who evaluate articles submitted to them are known to make decisions on whether the piece is worth their continued reading upon judging the development of the first paragraph. They know good writers can be identified early by their skill in using punctuation marks and capitalizing properly; and, as this can usually be determined early, they do not waste their time with pieces that seem to signal they will require a lot of editing prior to publication. Because this tendency is well known, writers commit themselves to displaying mastery of the rules governing punctuation and capitalization as a first priority. Even the best writers return to the rules that apply and to tips concerning them in cases where they are in doubt or confused.

Because I am convinced that writers should maintain portfolios that contain readily available guides to assist them in all writing chores, I have dedicated a great deal of my success program to the writing art. Due to my belief that individuals should be spared the time-consuming task of returning to English books in order to review how most punctuation marks are used, the list below, along with brief explanations of their uses, has been developed to serve as a quick reference guide for those who wish to better themselves in the writing department:

<u>Punctuation Essentials</u>

The importance of punctuating properly should not be overlooked because no writing is good if it is not clear, and no writing is clear if it is not well punctuated. Punctuation marks are essential to clear writing because they serve to package the meanings of words in usable clumps like phrases, clauses, and sentences. They also serve to assist the reader to feel as if he was listening to a speaker.

Terminal Marks: The standard terminal marks which are the *period*, the *question mark*, and the *exclamation mark* have the power to end a sentence; however, several others—the *dash*, the *colon*, and *ellipsis*—have this power *within* sentences that may or may not be complete. Wise individuals may turn to the reference library for clarification; however, the main features of the three standard terminal marks are as follows:

- <u>The Period</u> (.), the most common terminal mark, presents very few problems. The difficulties encountered are (1) in distinguishing between abbreviations that take and do not take periods, and (2) its use in relation to other marks of punctuation.

  Rules for these differences are covered clearly in reference library books.

- <u>The Question Mark</u> (?) is used at the end of a sentence that asks a direct question, or after titles of books, plays, etc., that ask questions.

- The Exclamation Point (!) is used to express strong feeling. It can be used after words, phrases, sentences, and when needed in titles, books, themes, etc.

Internal Marks: Other marks are used to introduce, separate, enclose, identify words spoken, indicate the possessive case, and lapses of time. While wise individuals work to understand their specific uses by consulting grammar and reference books; however, the general uses of these are as follows:

- The Comma (,) introduces, separates and encloses. It generally indicates a mild pause.
- The Semicolon (;) separates parts of the sentence that cannot be separated by a comma.
- The Colon (:) is used after a word introducing quotations, an explanation, a series, or a salutation in the formal letter; it is also used between time expressions (2:30 A.M., or a.m.) and ratios (1:2). (*The colon may also serve on occasion at the end of a sentence.*)
- The Dash (--) can perform the functions of introduction, separation, enclosure, and termination. (*While the dash is also listed as a non-standard terminal mark, It should not be used to take the place of another mark.*)
- Brackets ([ ]) enclose statements that are independent of the rest of the sentence, and parenthetical material inserted by someone other than the author.
- Parentheses [( )] while shown here in brackets, are used to enclose references and directions, figures and letters marking the order of a series, and expressions that cannot be set off by commas or dashes.
- Quotation Marks (" ") identify words spoken in direct discourse, and are used to set off quoted material.
- The Apostrophe (') is used to indicate the possessive case of nouns, the plural of letters and figures, and to denote the omission of letters in words like *"don't."*
- Points of Ellipsis (…) indicate an omission, a lapse of time, or a particularly long pause. (*ellipsis may also serve on occasion at the end of a sentence.*)
- The Hyphen (-) connects compound words, marks the division of a word at the end of a syllable that could not be completed; and is used to indicates breaks in phone, account numbers, etc., and to mark inclusive page numbers like *"pp. 29-40."*
- The Double Hyphen (--) is the same as the dash mark. When placed in a manuscript, a printer will transpose it into a longer "em" dash. It is often used in pairs, so it is the equivalent of parentheses, or even commas around a clause or phrase.
- The Asterisk (*) is used as a footnote reference when only a few such references are planned.
- The Bar Virgule (/) is a mark of separation and indicates the omission of words. The contraction of dates like *6/26/11* is not acceptable in formal writing.

Good Writers Seek To Master Capitalization Rules

In the same way that being able to punctuate skillfully is a distinguishing feature of good writers, so too is the ability to display capitalization skills. I believes that the capitalization rules are much easier to master than are the rules for punctuation because they are closely related to understanding the difference between proper nouns and common nouns. While specific names of persons, places, and things are proper nouns that must always be capitalized, and that the group to which the proper nouns relate are common nouns and are never capitalized. The following is intended to put these rules in a nutshell or those who intend to be proficient writers:

Capitalization Rules

- Proper nouns and abbreviations of proper nouns must be capitalized.
  (Reverend James T. Hooker; Rev. Hooker)

- Names and titles of relatives must be capitalized unless the specific names are preceded by a possessive pronoun.
  (Mother; my mother)

- Titles of office before a name, or used instead of the name, require capitalization.
  (President Obama will speak; the President is leaving.)

- Degrees and titles following the name are capitalized.
  (Evelyn Jordan, BS; Tommy Whitfield, Sr.)

- Positions of importance are capitalized.
  (Mayor of Houston; the Consular General of Mexico)

- Sections of the country are capitalized, but not directions.
  (The weather in the North and Northwest is colder; we get there by traveling north.)

- All references to the Deity, religious faiths, and books concerning them are capitalized.
  (God, BC, AD, Baptist, Catholic, the Bible)

- Names of specific organizations must be capitalized.
  (Highsmith Middle School; Boy Scouts of America)

- Historical documents and events are always capitalized.
  (The Gettysburg Address, The Civil War)

- Holidays, months of the year, days of the week, and their abbreviations are always capitalized.
  (Mothers' Day; July— Jul; Monday—Mon.)

- All languages must be capitalized.
  (English, Spanish, Latin, etc.)

- Academic Courses are capitalized, but not areas of study.
  (Mathematics 121; mathematics, psychology)

- Titles of plays, magazines, and published works must be capitalized. The first and last words of a title are always capitalized, and all words except articles, conjunctions, and short prepositions are capitalized.
  (Wall Street Journal; Webster's New Reference Library; Dancin' in the Street)

- The first word starting a direct quotation is always capitalized.
  (Professor Higgins said "Learning capitalization rules is easy"; "Just wait," he said, "you will see what I mean."

A Simple Letter To A Child – An Example

Greetings
Grades
Mother
Work and Play
Words
Close November 20, 20__

Dear Son,

I hope that you are well, and that you are missing me as I do you. I can hardly wait to shake your hand ; however, this letter gives me an opportunity to congratulate you on your most recent success and to mention a few things that should be brought to your attention as well.

I was pleased to learn of your excellent semester grades. Congratulations! Good grades are always expected of those with good minds, and all your this year seem to say that you are really committed to being a top student. To me this is great news! I understand that you are somewhat disappointed with the "B" in algebra, but that you are taking steps to find out and correct what was overlooked. I am very happy that this is your attitude. Keep up the good work!

Mother informs me that you have stepped in my shoes in taking out the garbage and keeping up the yard. She also let me know that you are helping out in other areas, including assisting your sister with chores and lessons. This is not only wonderful news, it assures me that you are beginning to understand that stepping out and helping loved ones are keys to successful and happy living. Needless to say, you are making me a very proud dad. Thanks!

Now Son, so that you will not think that we are encouraging you to always keep your nose to the grindstone with work and with lessons, I want to make our intentions clear. Since a good mind requires a healthy body, both your mother and I fully endorse your taking the time to exercise and have fun. These things are essential to your health, fitness, social ability, and being all-around. In other words— work, study, music, sports, reading, writing, and playing both mental and physical games, make for a wholesome person. You can depend on us, therefore, to support you in all such endeavors.

In supporting you at the moment, please notice the words I placed at the top part of this letter. I wrote them there for three reasons: First, because these are the topics I wanted to address in my letter to you. Second, by listing the points I wished to discuss, it keeps me on track and allows me to breeze through my letter with ease. (This technique will save you from taking over an hour to compose your monthly letters to Grandmother). The third reason is that I am hoping you will adopt a similar time saving system for developing your school papers. I believe this, the simplest form of outlining, will be as helpful as is the "Really Reading Concept" you have recently adopted.

I am looking forward to seeing all of you at the end of the month and getting a personal update from a son who pleases me immeasurably. In the meantime, please pass my warmest greetings to Mother and to my baby girl.

Much love,
Dad

Outlining Tips Worth Keeping

While the *topic outline* discussed by the child's dad in *"A Simple Letter To A Child"* may be useful in developing simple papers, expanding it to become a *sentence outline,* is deemed to be a stronger format because it contains a complete thought. In that the sentence outline is the format thought to be used by writers of note, *the biggest tip* aspiring writers need is to learn as much as possible about how to go about expanding topics for discussion into sentence outlines.

All authors utilize the outlining process for making their presentations coherent; writers of textbooks take special care in organizing their work so that it is presented in a logical manner.   This makes the outlining of textbook chapters an easy task for students who do so to fully understand the material. For students, the process of developing coherent and logically presented term, research papers, and other compositions to be turned is more complex because evaluators sometimes require that outlines be submitted along with compositions in order to evaluate the process used by the writer in structuring his work.

While details pertinent to the appearance of the outline are covered during the discussion of the Formal Outline (the next entry), the 3 tips below are intended to detail a manner of moving from the topic outline format to that of a sentence outline. For those aspiring to be improved in the writing arena, these tips are recommended to be kept in their portfolio on being better.

Tips on Preparing the Outline

1. Select the subject of your paper: a) decide on a general topic; b) survey resources, and c) write the thesis statement.

2. Make a rough draft of your outline: jot down at random all the points about your paper that come to mind, and group similar points together; decide what pattern would be best to follow (chronological, geographical, a study of contrasts or comparisons, cause or effect, or a study of influences); write a simple topic outline where you choose two to four important points for the major divisions, and place the remaining ideas as sub-topics under them. *You can then assess the result by considering: if you are fulfilling your thesis statement, if you have covered the subject adequately, and if the sub-topics fall logically under it larger topic. This will allow you to eliminate any material that does not fit, and determine if you need to look for additional information.*

3. Write the outline in final sentence form: word the main topics so they are clear, concise, and parallel (parallelism means using similar wording for various divisions of equal rank); fill in the sub-topics using the same criteria; and check to see that the outline is in correct outline form.

An Example Illustrating Parallelism

Wrong	Right
How to do the laundry	How to do the laundry

	Wrong		Right
I.	Sorting by colors	I.	Sorting by colors
II.	To start the machine	II.	Starting the machine
III.	Proper water temperature	III.	Choosing proper water temperature
IV.	How to handle delicate fabrics	IV.	Handling delicate fabric

The Formal Outline

Outlines in general, are as important to writers as are blueprints to builders, and as patterns are to those who make things. The formal outlining process is to a paper what a road map is to a journey because the thesis statement relates to your destination, and the divisions and form of the outline signal that you have planned to arrive at your destination safely. While used as a guide that can be modified as needed, good writers take pains to see that: 1) their map presents a picture can be easily followed, 2) that its divisions are consistent with a well organized paper, and 3) that the form of it is correct throughout. The information below concerning the basic guidelines for picture, form, and divisions will assist those who wish to develop outlines they can be proud of:

Picture Of An Outline

Title of Your Paper

Thesis Statement (It should pinpoint your objective exactly)

I. Major division

    A. Subdivision

        1. Sub-subdivisions
        a.
        (1)
            (a)
            (b)
        (2)
        b.

        2. Sub-subdivision

    B. Subdivision

II. Major division

Outlining Divisions

Roman Numeral Information must explain the thesis. If there is a Roman numeral I, there must be a Roman numeral II.

    Capital Letter Information must explain the Roman numeral above it. If there is a capital letter A, there must be a capital letter B.

    Arabic Numeral Information must explain the capital letter above it. If there is an Arabic numeral 1, there must be an Arabic numeral 2.

    Small Letter Information must explain the Arabic numeral above it. If there is a small letter "a," there must be a small letter "b."

<u>Form in Outlining</u>

Symbols (I., A., 1. a., etc.) —These are always punctuated with periods.

Statements—All begin with capital letters.

Topics—Topics are not punctuated.

Sentences—Sentences are always punctuated.

Lines—When more than one line is used in writing a statement, the first letter of the second line must come directly under the first letter of the line above it. Also, one line should be skipped before the next Roman numeral segment.

Spacing—The locations of symbols should be parallel with the same symbol above it, i.e., Roman numerals, capital letters, etc.; and the segment should be grammatically parallel, e.g., if the segment after capital A is a phrase or dependent clause, so should the segment after B, and after C and D, if used.

The Formal Letter

There are eight basic parts in the format of the formal letter. Social and personal letters are not formal in nature, and usually omit one or two of these parts, however, unless there are enclosures, proper business letters will be developed using all 8 parts. As explained in the reference library book that provides visual examples, some "official" letters require three additional parts.

Good writers pay particular attention to the eight standard parts of the formal letter, along with the additional letter, and are careful to include the additional parts needed in the formatting of their business and official letters.

Notes explaining the specific locations of these parts within letters in he formal category are shown below:.

<u>Parts of the Formal Letter</u> (**Set up in a** *block format*)

1. *Heading.* The writer's address is written or shown at the top of the sheet.
2. *Date Line.* All letters must be dated. The usual place is to the top and right, a line lower than the heading.
3. *Inside Address.* The name and address of the recipient of the letter is placed at this location. This address is placed flush with the left margin, four or five lines below the date line.
4. *Salutation.* This, the greeting line, is located 2 lines down, and is always followed by a colon.
5. *Body.* The part of the letter that carries the message. It begins 2 lines under the salutation.
6. *Complimentary Close.* The closing phrases, such as *Sincerely yours, Very truly yours*, etc., are placed 2 lines down from the last line of the body.
7. <u>Signature</u>. All letters must be signed by the writer. The written signature is 4 lines down from the complimentary closing, and is followed by a typed signature and the writer's position.
8. <u>Enclosure line</u>. When this line is used, it is located 2 lines under the typed writer's position, and may make note of the number of enclosures attached. (Enclosure) (Enclosures –2)

<u>Additional Letter Parts</u> (**Often found in business and official letters**)

- *Subject Line.* When used to Identify the topic of the letter, it is located 2 lines above the salutation.

- *Attention Line.* When used in letters to businesses, it is placed on the line just under the line designating the company being addressed in order to direct the letter to a particular person with a special interest in subject discussed,

- *Identification Initials.* These initials identify in the first position the person who dictated the letter, and the secretary who typed it in the second position (heb/cd). These initials are placed 2 lines below the last line of the letter flush with the left margin.

Paragraph Development

With the understanding that the purpose of the paragraph is to develop one idea, good writers choose the best way to prove, explain, illustrate, analyze or otherwise elaborate on the idea. When these writers understand that they are concerned with only three types of sentences; the one expressing the main idea, those that constitute the major portion of the paragraph in supporting this idea, and a concluding sentence that is sometimes used to restate the main idea, summarize and elaborate on the supporting details, or serve as a connector to the next paragraph.

Although understanding the anatomy of the paragraph, with respect to the types of sentences therein, is the first important requirement for those who wish to be better writers, I find it unfortunate that little emphasis is placed on paragraph development in regular education courses. Because I believe that this oversight is the primary cause of individuals struggling to write with confidence, my intention is to arm them with knowledge pertinent to the various ways that ideas can be presented easily.

In that I feel that when these individuals will be well on their way to being more skillful writers when the different ways in which paragraphs may be developed for presenting ideas clearly have been identified, and when concrete examples have been provided to clarify how these are projected. The first requirement is to understand that there are 7 common ways in which writers can develop their ideas. These are identified below:

7 Common Ways For Developing Paragraphs

1. *Developed by Simple Support.* Used when supporting sentences are available to give proof or evidence of the assertion made in the topic sentence.

2. *Developed by Examples or Illustrations.* Used when it is difficult to say or explain something clearly, and when one or more examples will provide images or pictures that are easy for another to understand. This technique is designed to get a point across more profoundly by telling a simple story using examples or illustrations that pertain to what a writer intends to share with readers.

3. *Developed by Process.* Used when making a procedure clear by explaining it in steps.

4. *Developed by Definition.* Used to more clearly explain or discuss an idea or concept by defining the word that embodies the idea. This way is effective when the definition expands the basic idea and when the information presented gives credence to the definition.

5. *Developed by Analogy.* Used to describe or explain a concept or thing by describing something quite different—but at the same time similar—so that there is a clear parallel between the two. Orwell, for example, used very human animals in his book, *"Animal Farm,"* to represent individuals who were somewhat less than human in their behavior.

6. *Developed by Comparison and Contrast.* Used when describing abstract ideas. In doing so, three forms are available:

      a. Showing comparisons or similarities

      b. Showing contrasts or dissimilarities

      c. Showing both comparisons and contrasts (combines the first two methods)

   7. *Developed by Reasons.* Used commonly to emphasize a high point by listing the reasons logically and in their increasing order of importance.

Developing Ideas—Examples Using The 7 Common Ways

> *Having a pattern for presenting ideas is the easiest way to develop them.*

While it is one thing to say that there are seven common ways in which a writer can develop an idea within a paragraph, those interested in a clearer understanding of how such is done in the practical realm may find themselves challenged. In my success program books, I not only provide this clarity by way of examples showing how such ideas are developed, but in utilizing the same theme, my intention is also to widen the horizons of my readers. This is also the expectation of the example paragraphs that follow. These were developed using the theme "Paragraphs On The Faces Of Pain."

1. *Paragraph Developed by Simple Support*

    I have developed a protective strategy to keep from being unhappy due to my failed dealings with others. Because being an unhappy person is a painful experience for me, I protect myself in a variety of ways. I associate only with folk who are positive, and avoid arguments of all kinds and at all times unless they are of the positive variety. Since I do not like to feel that I owe anyone, or that someone is indebted to me, I do not borrow; neither do I lend. This is because it seems that both of these vices usually lead to some promise or some heart being broken. When my advice is asked for, I will readily respond with a solution I think is best for solving the person's immediate problem; however, when I notice my advice is not taken, I am satisfied that my best advice was given and never do I attempt to involve myself in the solution again unless asked to do so. My method is to react to the requests of a family member or a friend promptly, but when I see that one's reaction to a request I make is less deliberate, or when one tends to show a lower grade of respect for me than I give him or her, I shut off my support, and refrain from involving that person in my affairs again. Being consigned to doing these few things protects me from even the minor bouts of agitation that may cause me anger or regret, and they help in keeping a smile on my face.

2. *Paragraph Developed by Example*

    My mother was an expert on teaching the sort of proper behavior that keeps others from being offended, distressed, and pained. When my brother and I both wanted a toy truck and tricycle for Christmas, she, knowing that there was not a great deal of money to go around, bought one truck and one tricycle, and taught us to share in playing with each. We were also urged to allow time for our visiting friends to play with our favorite toys as long as they wished. When we went on vacation, she was sure to take along toys of some sort that both my brother and I enjoyed, and a couple of interesting storybooks. When she noticed her boys' tempers getting out of hand when playing together, she always insisted on making one play alone for a period, while the other read a story from one of the books. But more than this, she taught us how to do a job well by way of demonstrating proper methods. Her urging us to keep uppermost in our minds the great idea of making sure the finished work was above the reproach of others, remains with me to this day. I believe this practice—making sure that work assignments met all inspection criteria—to be above all the other practices she encouraged so effortlessly.

3. *Paragraph Developed by Process*

I have an almost foolproof method of helping others understand that I will never be fully responsible for bringing them pain. The process is rather simple; however, the act of doing it takes a degree of guts. Almost anyone can do as I have done to keep others from the emotional distress engendered when they falsely think that I am the reason for their suffering. First, I tell those in my circle of friends and co-workers that they can depend on me to carry my share of the load at all times, and to treat them fairly and respectfully. Second, I continue by saying if they look at a situation properly, they will always find that I will never be fully responsible for any bad feeling they may harbor toward me. Then I tell them if at any time they find they are angry with me, to ask themselves why are they angry with me? I tell them whatever answer they come up with—like, for example, they are angry because I raised my voice or said something curt—that they should ask of themselves what drove me to do so? I drive my point home by telling them that in every case they will find that my reaction to them was caused by an earlier improper act on their part; and therefore, that they will be almost wholly responsible for bringing on the ensuing anger and pain they are feeling.

4. *Paragraph Developed by Definition*

From the dictionary we learn that the word "pain" is defined as an unpleasant sensation varying in severity, and resulting from injury, disease, or emotional disorder. It is defined also as suffering or distress. The point that pain, itself, has varying degrees of severity, informs us that the sense of pain has several forms or faces—all of which are unpleasant. Little boys and girls feel it when they skin their knees or have a toothache. Their mothers and fathers are pained upon observing the tears that flow from an injured child, and again when they apply a medication whose sharpness increases the hurt before soothing and healing it. Teachers are sometimes pained when their students fail to understand something that has been explained completely more than once. In the same way, one's friends have hurt feelings when teased, or when they have been snubbed in not receiving an invitation, etcetera. Although varying in degree, the fact that "unpleasantness" is the sensation felt in the painful situations mentioned, gives credence to its definition.

5. *Paragraph Developed by Analogy*

Pain, even the thought of it being brought to bear, is something that all creatures flee from at the earliest possible opportunity. It is closely akin to fear in that it brings about emotions that arise subjectively rather than through conscious effort. A man who wishes to escape the tyranny of jeers from peers who belittle his ideas, goes into seclusion in some hidden habitat. When he wishes to avoid the pain of envy from another who may covet his wife or his possessions, a man builds a high wall around his residence. In a battle, for fear of receiving injuries or death, some men refuse to fight and cowardly hide themselves or flee the battle scene. Instead of a war declaration, even powerful countries have been known to resort to sneak attacks against an unsuspecting neighbor as a way of avoiding pain that may come somehow to them. Some cultures, in order to avoid the pain of another culture being mixed with theirs, resort to eradication or annihilation of the race that is weaker in war-fighting ability. In the same way, and—perhaps for some of the same reasons—animals, insects, and fowl, are known to dig holes, construct webs, and build nests in places that offer security for themselves and difficulty for their potential adversaries.

We see the similarity between man and beast again in their fighting instincts, whereby some defend their territories against all comers courageously, while some—like the cowardly hyena—will only attack in packs or hordes to overcome a defenseless prey who, in fear of pain, injury, or death, can only run away.

6. *Paragraph Developed by Comparison and Contrast*

Although similar, there is a difference in the sensations of pain and pang. One, *pain*, has to do with an unpleasant sensation varying in severity, and resulting from injury, disease, or emotional disorder; while *a pang* also having to do with such a sensation varying in its severity, its defining quality has to do with suddenness— as in *"a sharp spasm of pain"*; or with a sharp feeling of emotional distress, as in *"the pang of childbirth."* Another way in which they differ is that *pain* is associated with sensations brought on by injury, disease, etc., while *a pang* can only be associated with these if the pain involved is sudden and spasmodic. Other than one having a longer-lasting effect than the other, the most positive difference between pain and pang is centered in the degree the mental aspects of the sensation is quantified or weighed in both. This quantity is embodied in the terms *"emotional disorder"* as applied to pain, and in *"emotional distress"* as applied to pang. After investigation of these terms, it is clearly evident that *distress* (to cause strain, anxiety or suffering) has to be seen as inferior to that of *disorder* which covers persons suffering from confusion or disarray, or from those who are ill physically or mentally. While there may be other differences, those mentioned so far exposes sufficiently the distinct difference between the sensations of pain and pang.

7. *Paragraph Developed by Reasons*

People deal uncomfortably with the dread of pain for various and sundry reasons. For some, the dread of being criticized causes them mental anguish beyond description. Many of our young refuse to follow advice that they know is sound because of the pain they feel arising from the idea that they would be forsaking their own uniqueness in following someone else's pattern. As far as individuals go, it is not difficult to connect pain-avoidance with the idea of overeating, shopping excessively and hoarding, and even alcohol and drug addiction. This is borne out by the pangs and the pains many alcoholics with D.T.'s *(delirium tremens)* experience, for what they want most to quiet the raging aches within them is another drink. In a still more serious vein, the mere worshipping by others of a god called by a different name is too much for some individuals and sects to bear, and they resort to atrocities in attempts to exact the vengeance they believe is called for. Our world history is replete with incidents of patricide and genocide in order to escape or avoid the pain of having to follow the just rule of another, or of having to live alongside another thought to be inferior. Even in this present day in our own country, many of our elected officials forego the act of representing the will of their constituents due to the pain they are unable to endure because of built-in personal biases. In many cases, politicians feel they are unable to endure the loss of personal gain, and in too many of these cases these representatives have replaced the loyalties owed their fellows with selfish loyalties to lobbying enterprises. In all cases, the dread of pain, whether personal, regional, or national, tends to effect not only the ones who wish to avoid it, but countless others who, for the most part, are innocent by-standers. While unfortunately, this is the horror of pain-avoidance, it is safe to say that it is just about impossible for one to escape this life without feeling this sensation due to the various and sundry reasons mentioned.

The Three-Paragraph Theme

By definition alone it is clear that the three-paragraph theme is a written composition whereby the space for developing it is limited. While normally assigned to students as a writing exercise, it is clear that the term " theme" suggests that the exercise is assigned to address a dominate or central idea. In that this work is like an artistic short speech, it, like all compositions, is required to have a beginning, middle, and end. While these are embodied in the phases—introduction, body, and conclusion, good writers take care not to label or set these phases apart by mentioning them in their papers.

In developing the theme, the writer's orientation is like unto the development of the paragraph where the central issue is introduced and supported; however, while the paragraph may not always have a concluding sentence, a concluding paragraph is necessary for closing out the issue being discussed in this composition. In order to demonstrate that they understand the criteria for constructing each of 3 paragraphs of the theme, good writers need not only to show their skill in developing paragraphs, but also to show how this skill is employed in utilizing 3 paragraphs only to deal with a central theme.

The following is intended to assist those who would be good writers by explaining the purposes of the 3 paragraphs utilized in developing the theme paper, and by providing tips for insuring each paragraph they devise will soundly meet the standard criteria established for evaluating it.

- Paragraph 1

In the first paragraph, the writer introduces the theme and provides a road map that guides the rest of the paper through its final destination. The introduction should (1) arouse the reader's interest; (2) make his position clear on the subject chosen; and (3) use a number of sentences to point out some general information to let the reader know about the subject he will develop. TIP: The writer should conclude the first paragraph by again expressing a statement of his thesis.

- Paragraph 2

The topic sentence in the middle paragraph or in the body of the composition should link what was stated in the introduction with what is to follow. The sentences in this paragraph must develop, support, explain, and give credence to the position stated in the introductory paragraph. It should include specific examples, readings, experiences, or details that back up the thesis. TIP: The writer should take pains to see that back-up information is appropriate and presented in a logical manner.

- Paragraph 3

The writer's objective in the concluding paragraph of the paper is that of summarizing and showing how the supporting details of the second paragraph served to clinch the main points of the thesis statement. In other words, it should evidence that he proved his point. TIP: The writer never introduces new evidence in this paragraph, nor does he use the words *"In conclusion."* His conclusion should be a statement expanding on his original theme.

PART 3

'RITHMETIC

While it is thought that the person when connecting the 3 R's with the foundational aspect of intelligence, was not referring to mathematics per se, but of skills for figuring out and coping with some important issues of life. Thinking on this order could very well be based on a belief that in the same way a person could take the single dimensional art of reading and writing to higher levels, the same person could also take the four dimensional components of basic arithmetic—addition, subtraction, multiplication, and division—to higher levels of usefulness in expressing an aspect of intelligence, and in making for a purposeful and profitable life.

The 4 items extracted from my success books for this part of the chapter go hand in hand with the need for one to have a general understanding of how forms of addition, subtraction, multiplication and division offer a disciplined thinking approach that can be utilized for showing one's acuteness in avoiding problems. This idea goes hand in hand with my belief that the true marks of those who are committed to improving themselves are shown by their skill in planning to make their lives less cumbersome. In my opinion, this is done by showing that they have figured out how to utilize semi-mathematical measures for empowering themselves; circumventing and making problems less onerous; developing procedures for saving time, energy, and resources; and combining these in a way that sets themselves apart from others.

This, then, is the reason for my selection of the four items below. These are intended to serve those who wish to better themselves in utilizing the wisdom I attribute to the person who first connected the 3 R's with the foundational aspects of intelligence.

- In <u>Goal Setting</u>, the value of setting both lifetime and intermediate goals is discussed. While the notes pertaining to assessing both personal and organizational goals, it may be said that the act of setting goals is a key addition to one's self-improvement portfolio.

- In <u>Permanent Records Worth Keeping</u>, a list of important documents that one will more than likely have to refer back to from time to time are shown and discussed. The point being emphasized is that one can take action to subtract from future worries by reserving records that pertain to past personal, schooling, business, employment, and travel concerns, and by maintaining a special place for storing them.

- The <u>Example 3 -Month Calendar</u> is intended to serve as a useful tool for planning personal and organizational activities, and for insuring that the division of participant labors are divided and that attention of participants is not divided.

- In <u>Quotes About Money</u>, the 13 quotes listed are intended to encourage you to think less about the acquisition and multiplication of monetary assets, but more about these in the broad sense of the forward thinkers whose quotes seem to be time-binding.

Goal Setting

<u>General</u>. Setting and meeting goals are important activities for persons who wish to employ checks and balances that add to the ideal of achieving their dreams. The reasons for doing so are:

- They give you long term and short term objectives to focus on.
- They point out areas on which to concentrate your mental and physical efforts.
- They identify choices available, and encourage proper decision-making.
- They serve as self-motivating devices.
- They build self-confidence and self-esteem.
- They encourage good practices that become habit forming.

<u>Setting Lifetime Goals</u>. Setting lifetime goals should always precede other goals because they serve as topic headings for the chapters describing the dreams for one's life. Lifetime goals pertain to the essential thoughts one has concerning what kind of person he or she wants to be, what this person wants to have accomplished by retirement age, and how he or she wishes to be seen by others. They come first because they constitute the central theme to be developed in the supporting chapters outlining the person's major goals, and they tend to help guide the development of the short-term goals that are essential to the completion of each dream.

While lifetime goals may change as situations change, the following list of questions were developed as guides for those who are far-seeing:

- What is the personal image I have projected for seeing myself in the future?
- How do I wish to be seen by others?
- How important is education to my dream?
- What kind of career do I wish to pursue?
- What kind of earning capacity do I wish to have?
- Do I plan on having a family?
- Am I concerned about being seen as a good citizen?

Setting Intermediate Goals. Intermediate goals are set to compliment the larger lifetime goals. They assist in establishing sets of important sub-goals, and in determining the amount of attention, time, and the help of others that will be necessary for goal attainment. It is recommended that these goals, divided into short-range or mid-range goals, be clearly described in writing, and revisited often in order to insure that they continue to meet the criteria for evaluating all established goals.

While the same criteria checks are used for personal and organizational goals, the questions following the six criteria items below should be asked by individuals upon assessing the goals they have established:

- *Realistic/Relevant:* ("Is it sensible and pertinent to one of my life goals?")

- *Practical:* ("Is it something that can be experienced, or is it just visionary?")

- *Attainable:* ("Can it be achieved primarily through my efforts, or are others necessary?")

- *Valuable:* ("Will it repay the time and effort I spend on making it a reality?")

- *Measurable:* ("Can I easily determine the amount of progress made?")

- *Time-bound:* ("Can it be accomplished within the time frame I established for its completion?")

Permanent Records Worth Keeping

A special place should be reserved for records that most individuals will more than likely have to refer back to in dealing with 21st Century issues. Because they are important documents, the personal records identified below are essential in the century's economy and workplace. Because having them on hand subtracts from future worry, doubt, and helplessness, they are also worthy of being kept safe in a designated place in the home.

Birth Certificate

Social Security Information

Transcripts

Schools and Colleges
(Include dates attended)

Diplomas, etc.

(Make copies)

Residences
(Include addresses of all homes and residences with move-in and move-out dates)

Jobs
(Include job titles with business addresses and names and numbers of employers and supervisors)

<u>Resumes</u>
(Include written notes developed to update future resumes)

<u>Major Purchases</u>
(List dates of purchase)

<u>Licenses</u>
(Make copies of each)

<u>Medical</u>
(Include insurance policies)

<u>ID Cards</u>
(Make copies of ID and credit cards)

<u>Passport</u>
Example 3-Month Calendar

Keeping and updating a calendar is a must for all who wish to build reputations for being timely and thoughtful. This activity is such a hallmark in businesses and in some organizations a staff person is designated to keep the calendar current. While parents use them to insure that they are on time for appointments, for paying bills, to support children's programs, and to schedule mandatory family outings, they are ideal for student use in recording dates for examinations and assignments due. I believe that multiple month calendars should be a mainstay for those whose job performances are dependent on dividing their time wisely and timely reporting. I believe also that their use is fundamental for all who wish to set themselves apart as dependable and trustworthy.

Jan 20__

Sunday	Monday	Tuesday	Wednesday	Thursday	Friday	Saturday
2	3	4	5	6	7	8
9	*[1]					15
16		*[2]				22
23						29
30	31					

Feb 20__

Sunday	Monday	Tuesday	Wednesday	Thursday	Friday	Saturday
		1	2	3	4	5
6						12
13 [3]						19
20						26
27	28			31		

Mar 20___

Sunday	Monday	Tuesday	Wednesday	Thursday	Friday	Saturday
		1	2	3	4	5
6						12
13						19
20						26 **[4]**
27	28 [5]	29	30 **[6]**	31		

(See explanation below for January 10 and 18; Feb 13; March 26, 28, and 30.)
[1] – House Inspection   [2] – Pay club dues   [3] – Family day   [4] – Petey's party, 7:00 p.m.
[5] –Susan's Birthday [6] – Golf at Seaside Resort, 1:15 p.m.

Quotes About Money

Multiplying your knowledge about how money is valued

Benjamin Franklin: "He that goes a borrowing goes a sorrowing."

Jim Cramer: "I wish it grew on trees, but it takes hard work to make money."

Paul Clitheroe: "There are plenty of ways to get ahead. The first is so basic that I am almost embarrassed to say it: 'Spend less than you earn.'"

David Bach: "Financial education needs to be a part of our national curriculum and scoring systems so that it is not just the rich kids that learn about money, it's all of us."

Barach Obama: "Focusing your life on making a buck shows a poverty of ambition. It asks too little of yourself, and will leave you unfulfilled."

Franklin D. Roosevelt: "Happiness is not the mere possession of money; it lies in the joy of achievement, in the thrill of creative effort."

Izaak Walton: "Look to your health; and if you have it, praise God, and value it next to a good conscious; for health is the second blessing that we mortals are capable of; a blessing money cannot buy."

Marian Wright Edelman: "Never work just for money or power. They won't save your soul or help you sleep at night."

Mohandas K. Gandhi: "Capital as such is not evil; it is the wrong done to us because of it that is evil. Capital in some form of other will always be needed."

<u>Thomas Wolfe</u>: "You have reached the pinnacle of success as soon as you become uninterested in publicity, compliments, and money."

<u>Eli Broad</u>: "There is no substitute for knowledge. To this day I read three newspapers a day. It is impossible to read a paper without being exposed to ideas. And ideas—more than money—are the real currency for success."

<u>Peter's Almanac</u>: "Early to bed and early to rise, 'til you get enough to do otherwise."

<u>The Author</u>: "Credit card companies have little use for people who pay off their entire bill on time each month. They prefer clients they can collect late payments on, and those who in making minimum payments, sometimes pay twice the value of the product when they charged it originally. Wise individuals know that it is time stop putting charges on a credit card when it becomes necessary to make a minimum payment."

CHAPTER V

ON THE ART OF SPEAKING WELL

Selling yourself and your ideas

Speaking before an audience has always been a very fearsome task for individuals who have not mastered the art of giving speeches. While mastery is expected only of speakers who have been highly trained, or those with a great deal of experience, it begins with learning about what makes speeches good or bad. Although several things are said to constitute a bad speech, there is widespread agreement that speeches are really bad when they do not present the message clearly and when speakers have annoying or distracting speaking habits. On the other hand, the main requirement of good speeches is that they be, well organized messages that are supported by evidence that is clearly presented. speakers are considered good when they are careful to maintain eye contact with their audience, insert interest-getting devices, and when they take pains to maintain control of both their voice and the speed in which the message is delivered.

In that the art of speaking well is best exampled by high paid TV and radio commentators, much can be learned by observing their methods, styles, their mastery of the language. Although the tips provided in this chapter are intended to address the artfulness required in making good speeches, its main focus is to provide information pertinent to the make-up and delivery of good speeches, and to encourage you to adopt standard formats for organizing your presentations.

While I understand that entire spectrum of speaking well cannot be covered in just a few pages, I have chosen 3 three items from my success program to meet this chapter's goals. I feel that when the essence of the articles below is included in the knowledge arsenals of those who wish to be better all-around, they will become more stimulating conversationalists, and will set themselves apart from their contemporaries in the arena of speaking well.

In *What Good Speakers Do*, a list of nine things that impact on the development and presentation of their topics in an effective manner is explained, and a set of tips on the process of organizing the speech is provided.

In On A Basic Format For Speaking, the purpose of the grammatical units that are basic to presenting ideas clearly, are reviewed; and information pertinent to formatting the three parts of most oral presentations is provided. This information is intended to be useful in communicating statements in informal settings, delivering a speech, and in presenting a class. Although the note at the end of this section is on formal speaking, it is occasions, is considered a worthwhile tip for speakers at any occasion..

In <u>Formats for Reporting</u>, both the standard and action reporting format are discussed. These formats, along with notes, are provided to not only serve as timesaving devices, but also as necessary aids for all who wish to give clear, concise, and complete reports.

What Good Speakers Do

1. Good speakers select topics they have given a great deal of thought to, or that they are very familiar with, such as: a concept, hobby, a procedure, or a plan.
2. They keep their ideas simple and always pertaining to the main theme, and are careful to stay within their time limitations in order to maintain their effectiveness.
3. They use words, phrases, and sentence structures that are familiar to their audiences because they know that their talk will have more impact when it is readily understood.
4. They clarify their concepts by examples and illustrations.
5. Although they understand an outline is a necessity for developing a coherent speech, they make short reminder notes consistent with the order of their ideas to be presented on cards, and practice presenting the speech using these notes. After going over the difficult passages from 10 to 20 times, they can make their points referring only to the reminder notes.
6. If the speech must be read, they plan to speak slowly and keep eye contact with their audience by looking up often in order to maintain rapport with all in attendance.
7. They stand erect, fully enunciate their words, and use conventional gestures when needed to emphasize their points and to keep the audience's attention.
8. They practice volume control using low, normal, and loud voices when needed.
9. When they think they are ready, they use a tape recorder during their practice sessions. Afterwards, they listen to themselves to see if changes are to be made. If so, they practice these changes in their practice sessions so the right words are ready when they need them.

<u>Tips On Organizing The Speech</u>

Good speakers organize their speeches using the three-part outline in developing the opening, body, and closing portions of their remarks. When preparing the outline, however, *they begin with the body*. If dealt with first, it will be easier to add the beginning and the end.

<u>The Opening</u>: You must first make mention of the introduction received, and say something briefly about the person who gave the introduction. The opening is where you get the audience's attention and on board with you and your message. This may be done in several ways, for example: a personal experience, a story that is humorous, an anecdote, a startling statement, or a rhetorical question.

<u>The Body</u>: This is where you drive home the message with a variety of strategies that fit. These may include the various ways in which ideas are presented, i.e., by simple support, illustrations or examples, reasons, procedures or steps, analogies, and comparisons and contrasts,.

<u>The Closing</u>: This is the point where you persuade your audience to agree, think, or act. Audiences remember and respond to challenges, so if you want them to do something, tell them. Always end your speech exactly as you had planned, then sit down.

On A Basic Format For Speaking

It is rather intriguing that when comments are made about a speech that has been delivered, one of its 3 parts and the ideas presented in each is focused on. Since this is the case, it would seem that it is essential that speakers ought to return to the basic premise learned in the earliest English classes concerning the grammatical units utilized in presenting ideas. By this is meant returning to the purpose of both the sentence and the paragraph as highlighted in an earlier chapter:

- The purpose of a sentence is to express a complete thought.
- A sentence is made up of two parts; a subject and a predicate, wherein:
  -- The subject is the theme or topic.
  -- The predicate is the verb of verbal phrase asserting something about the subject including complements, objects, and modifiers.

- The purpose of a paragraph is to develop one idea.
- The paragraph is developed by employing 3 classifications of sentences, wherein:
  -- The topic sentence states the main idea.
  -- The supporting sentences embellish on the main idea by providing examples, explanations, details, etc.
  -- The concluding sentence, when used, may serve to restate the main idea, summarize the supporting details, or act as a linking agent to the next paragraph.

We can gather from this that the sentence format is utilized in presenting every worthwhile statement—meaning that it contains a subject, along with clarifying information that expands on the subject; and likewise, when expressing ideas clearly each must be introduced, supported, and brought to an end. It follows, using this logic, that whether one is responding to a question, giving a speech, presenting a class, or in making a report, a format based on paragraph development skills comes in handy if one is to do so skillfully.

Although it will be seen that formats for making reports are somewhat different, the point made at this juncture is that paragraph development is the essential skill needed in presenting ideas during speaking engagements. It follows that this skill is essential in developing the 3 main parts of all semi-formal and formal speaking engagements. These are:

1. The Introduction – the preliminary treatment leading to the topic's development.
2. The Body – the main part of the discourse.
3. The Conclusion – the last part delivered in a variety of ways; among these:
   a. The end or last part of a discourse, often containing *a summary* of what went before (*Summary*: the substance of a general idea in brief form).
   b. The last step in the reasoning process; or in forming a judgment, decision, or an opinion, after investigation or thought.
   c. The last of a chain of events about the subject.
   d. The 3rd part of a syllogism (*Syllogism*: an argument or form of reasoning in which 2 statements or premises are made, and a logical conclusion is drawn from them.) Example: (1) "All mammals are warm-blooded animals." (2)

"Whales are mammals." (3) "Therefore, whales are warm-blooded."

A speaker, armed with this basic format, needs only to understand the nature of these parts and how they are employed differently in accordance with the audience being addressed. These differences are shown in the examples below that spell out how they may be used when the speaker is: 1) making a simple statement or report, 2) giving a speech, and 3) presenting a class.

Regarding Part 1 - The Introduction:
- In *a simple statement or report*, the topic sentence may serve as the introduction.
- In *a speech*, the introduction may be concerned with platitudes—commonplace remarks —and with the topics to be discussed.
- In *presenting a class*, the introduction may consist of attention statement, topic, purpose, and the learning objectives.

Regarding Part 2—The Body:
- In *a simple statement or report*, the body may consist of supporting details that backup the topic sentence.
- In a speech, the body may be developed along lines that support the speaker's reasoning.
- In *a class presentation*, the body should consist of explanations, examples, details, etc., for the purpose of developing the learning objectives.

Regarding Part 3—The Conclusion:
- In *a simple statement or report*, the concluding sentence may serve to end it.
- In a speech, the speaker may choose to summarize, to make clear that the details presented have led to the conclusion that his original objective asserted, or he may choose to just leave the audience with a final thought.
- In *a class presentation*, the conclusion, at a minimum, should consist of a summary, a review of learning objectives, a check-up to see that the objectives were met, and a closing statement.

Formal Speaking

Effective formal speakers take care to speak on topics of real interest to the audience being addressed, and they always use well-developed notes to guide their practice sessions. During practice they take pains to evaluate their notes in order to determine if certain thoughts are presented clearly, if they should be discarded, or if there are more appropriate ways to project the idea in question. While they may utilize reminder notes instead of their originally developed notes, these speakers take care to avoid getting off message and taking chances that may lead to their exceeding their time limitations or being clumsy when adding to or expounding on topics they have not planned to discuss.

Formats For Reporting

Professionals in every walk of life will at some time be concerned with the act of giving and receiving reports. For many, reporting itself is a profession, e.g.: news reporting, financial reporting, business reporting, weather reporting, and accident reporting. Professionals in the legal, medical, and financial fields must use and be familiar with a variety of reporting forms; however, since these vary with the requirements of their offices, it behooves the individuals involved to assemble the type reports that pertain to their areas of interests, and maintain them in readily available files.

I recommend that professionals maintain written copies of expertly developed reports utilized in their crafts, and that these and others have on hand ready mental formats for giving accurate reports of all kinds. I believe that individuals of all types who wish to display good reporting skills will do well to arm themselves with formats for the two types of reports they usually give and receive. When armed with both formats, success-oriented individuals will not only be more expert in giving wholesome reports, but more expert in determining whether or not the reports they receive are complete. For this reason, the memory keys shown below have been developed for recalling the topic headings for both types of reports: *Standard Reports* and *Action reports*.

The standard reporting format can be used at any time. It consists of 6 questions, that, when answered, provide salient information. Known universally as the "5 W's"; a memory cue for this format is "5 W's and How." As will be seen, it is readily adaptable to modify the actionreporting format.

- **W**ho? – *Who was involved?*

- **W**hat? – *What happened?*

- **W**hen?—*What day and time did this occur?*

- **W**here? – *Where did this incident take place?*

- **W**hy? – *If known, why did this happen?*

- **H**ow?—*If known, how did it occur?*

While it is not necessary to follow the exact order listed above, skilled reporters make mention of the questions they have no responses for, and keep written versions of all their reports.

The action reporting format, borrowed from military annals for reporting tactical information, is a useful tool for the astute reporter. The acronym, SALUTE, serves as a memory cue for the questions in this format.

- **S**ize? (*How many?*) [5 male and 1 female student were observed.]

- **A**ctivity? (*What were they doing?*) [Accosting unnamed male student.]

- **L**ocation? (*Where was this taking place?*) [In the hallway in front of room 202.]

- **U**nit? (*What organization, if known was involved?*) [These are reported to be members of the XYZ gang.]

- **T**ime? (*When did this happen?*) [It began at 2:15 p.m., and lasted for 5 minutes.]

- **E**quipment? (*Were weapons or fighting objects observed?*) [3 of the gang members were brandishing knives; one, the biggest of the lot, had a baseball bat.]

CHAPTER VI

ON DECISION MAKING AND PROBLEM SOLVING

Getting the upper hand

Decision-making—the act of making up one's mind. It is a process where one course of action is selected from a few possible alternatives.

Problem-solving – the act of finding a solution that best resolves the issue. It is a process where the ultimate goal is to overcome the obstacles involved.

A parent of one of my students prompted me to develop a short study on decision-making and problem-solving. This happened when I was coordinator of Houston ISD's Career Academy, a high school program for students at-risk of not completing their educational studies successfully. In a parent-teacher conference, I asked this mother why she would allow her child to come to school dressed inappropriately and to enroll in an honors course that she would have obvious difficulty in completing? The mother replied, *"I let that girl make decisions on little things like that."* Needless to say I gave her an earful. Among the points I made were: 1) that this 15 yearold child had not made a *decision* in these cases, but a *choice* that were not based on thinking about the advantages of other courses of action open to her; and 2) that it was her responsibility to not go along with choices that would obviously be troublesome.

By the end of this meeting, I was convinced that the problem in this case dealt with the mother not understanding her responsibility for helping her child in making proper decisions. In thinking that she and many others of my parents would benefit from a serious conversation on decision-making and problem-solving, I decided to make these topics a focal point for discussion at the next monthly meeting with the academy's parent support group. In that my short talk with this group was enthusiastically received, it became clear to me lessons on these topics should be given long before one's high school years. I feel these lessons should begin with definitions such as are captured at the top of this page

Although entire books have been dedicated to discussing both topics together due of their relatedness, I believe they should be introduced early on in the educational arena; however, in a condensed and simplified form. While I believe students and others will be better off if given a separate understanding of each, I think it is imperative for those who are committed to being better to be armed with the steps involved in dealing intellectually with both. Even then, it is my view that the importance of developing decision-making skills cannot be overstated because they come into play in almost all one does, including the act of simple problem solving.

In this chapter I have called upon my military and other experiences to develop a short study to clarify the processes for dealing with both easy to solve and the more complex varieties of problems and tasks. Of the three pieces selected for this chapter, the first two deal with the formatting process. I believe that individuals armed with these will have a definite edge on their less informed contemporaries. The third piece *is* intended to provide information not found in the literature on these important topics, but that decision-makers will do well to employ when developing either simple and complex action plans.

Although these are condensed versions, when taken together they represent what I believe to be the necessary critical thinking tools needed for dealing with problematic issues of all types, and what I believe to be essential for those on the road to being exceptional decision makers and problem solvers. The formats are aptly named:

- *"The 3 Steps Necessary in Simple Problem Solving"*
- *"The 5-Part Decision-making Format,"*
- *"Notes Pertinent To Decision-making and Problem-solving"*

The 3 Steps Necessary In Simple Problem Solving

Step 1. <u>State the problem</u> (Identify the thing needing to be fixed and tell how it occurred).

Step 2. <u>Determine the facts and those things that bear on the problem</u> (If the things that bear negatively on the problem cannot be eliminated altogether, they must be given full attention during study of the options available).

Step 3. <u>Solve the problem</u> (Make a decision based on the best options).

<u>Solving a Simple Problem – An Example</u>

<u>Step 1</u>. (*State the problem*) The problem being faced is whether or not to allow my child to enter kindergarten at age 5.

<u>Step 2</u>. (*Determine the facts and those things that bear on the problem*) The facts that bear on this problem are several:

    a. My child will turn 5 only a few days before the opening day; however she is precocious and is anxious to begin her schooling.

    b.   My child is small for her age, and has not learned to stand up for herself.

    c.   My child cries easily when she does not get her way.

<u>Step 3</u>. (*Solve the problem*) With regard to the options available—to enroll her in kindergarten or to wait until she is 6—it seems best under the circumstances to wait until the time she will be older, a little bigger, and is a bit more mature in dealing with others.

The 5- Part Decision-Making Format

This 5-part format is recommended for use in dealing with both individual and organizational assignments and tasks. While the italicized notes below in parenthesis are intended to explain each of the parts, the questions following each part are considered most important in dealing with the part being addressed.

<u>Part 1</u>. The task or objective. (*The task or problem*)

<u>Important Questions</u>:

a. In considering the objective, are there some non-stated, implied task(s) that ought to be considered?

b. In what way does the time to make a decision affect how I would normally plan to deal with this situation?

<u>Part 2</u>. The Situation and Courses of Action (C/A) Available. (*What is happening now? How many different ways can this issue be dealt with?*)

<u>*Important Questions:*</u>

a. What changes to the situation, if any, are anticipated before action begins?

b. Which C/A is best to deal with the task or problem? Example: (C/A #1: Proceed to the objective head-on); (C/A #2: Go around or over the major trouble spots); (C/A #3: By-pass one or more trouble spots; however deal with the ones that impede success).

<u>Part 3</u>. Consideration of Opposing Courses of Action. (*The major obstacle(s) in the way that may impede progress*).

<u>*Important Questions:*</u>

a. What major resistance is anticipated, and what obstacles can I expect to be placed in my way as I proceed to the intermediate objective and the final objective?

b. How can resistant forces and obstacles in my way be dealt with easiest?

Part 4. <u>Analysis of own courses of action</u>. (*Analysis of the advantages or disadvantages presented in taking courses of action #1, #2, and 3*).

<u>Important Question:</u>
Considering safety, speed, and the conservation of resources, which course of action offers the best chance of success?

Part 5. Decision/Recommendation Statement. (*The statement arrived at after considering all aspects of Parts 1 through 4 of the format*).

<u>Important Question:</u>
How is this statement different if rendered in the individual and organizational settings?
(*If used to resolve an individual's problem, he decides which C/A is best and the time it is to be started; however, if used resolve an organizational problem, he renders he decision arrived at as a formal recommendation.* <u>Notes Pertinent To Decision-making and Problem-solving</u>

Although many of the decisions made daily have little, if anything, to do with problems, it is a fact that and all problem-solving efforts are concerned with decision-making. In viewing the world around us, it is obvious that improper, mediocre, and even poor decisions are the reasons for problems not being resolved and for plans not succeeding. In light of the fact that making decisions is one of the most important of all mental activities, success-oriented persons will do well to understand that: a decision has more than one face; decisions fall into two general categories; and that decision-makers should test the soundness of both personal and business decisions.

The Two Faces of Decisions

It should be understood that the solutions arrived at using the decision-making process at certain levels within an organization or at the request of others are not always referred to as decisions. When made by subordinates and presented to others, their decisions are called *recommendations*. Likewise, in the case of a spouse, he or she understands that in making decisions that affect the family, as a family partner, the decisions or choices selected are submitted to the other spouse as a recommendation.

The Two Categories of Decisions

It is generally true that both simple and complex decisions fall into two categories: 1) those that affect relationships with individuals and things that fall into your "My and Our" categories, and 2) those that bear on the expenditures of your and organizational resources of time, money, equipment, materials, facilities, and supplies. And while it may seem that these categories pertain to separate personal and business interests, in many cases they are intertwined; therefore, it behooves success-oriented persons to adopt a foolproof format for testing their decisions. *An Infallible Decision Tester*

The following, taken from the Principles of War (symbolized by the military acronym (OMOMSSSUE), may be modified by decision-makers to determine the soundness of the major decisions made:

- **O**bjective—(*Does this decision go to the heart of the problem?*)

- **M**aneuver—(*Does this decision allow time and space to get things done?*)

- **O**ffensive—(*Does this decision allow me to move always toward the objective?*)

- **M**ass—(*Does this decision allow me to concentrate my efforts at the proper time?*)

- **S**ecurity—(*Is this decision one is oriented toward safety?*)

- **Si**mplicity—(*Will this decision be easily understood by those participating in the action contemplated?*)

- **S**urprise—(*Have I considered worst-case scenarios in making this decision?*)

- **U**nity of Command—(*Is this decision specific in insuring that changes to it can only be made only by the principal leader?*)

- **E**conomy of Force—(*Does this decision allow me to conserve the use of power until additional power is needed?*)

Key Decision-making and Problem-solving Notes

The following, in the form of questions, are considered essential for fool-proofing most decisions made for solving problems and for dealing with action plans that may involve others, obstacles to overcome, environmental conditions, facilities, and communications:

Others: Who is available to help out, and with what amounts of support? How much time is available to get these folk, to include their equipment, materials, supplies, etc., assembled and ready for action?

Obstacles: What obstacles, physical and human, am I most likely to face and have to overcome in order to achieve success?

The Environment: What effect will predicted weather have on movement and travel while accomplishing the assigned and implied tasks? (The *"weather"* aspect may refer also the temperament (hot, warm, cold) of individuals that are, or that may become, involved in the task or problem to be resolved.)

Facilities: is room available to house the materials and other resources needed, or will it be necessary to request additional space?

Communications: What communications means will be used --letters telephone, fax, messenger, face-to-face meetings, or combinations of these? Will there be a need for back-up communication modes?

CHAPTER VII

ON MANAGEMENT
AND LEADERSHIP

Setting yourself apart as an effective manager and leader

Strangely enough, while many individuals are raised to positions of authority and given roles as managers and leaders due to having gained special knowledge of an organization's operations, too many of these are unable to speak with coherence about the nature of their positions, nor of the principles used to guide them in playing their functional roles in these positions. This may well be due to the fact that the emphasis is mainly on theory analysis in universities and training schools, and not on the practical aspects of the profession being addressed. Although most individuals holding authoritative positions are unlikely to fall short in meeting expectations at their present levels of employment, it is felt that when given positions that require them to build up other managers and leaders, they will fall short if they are not armed with certain key information that is usually overlooked in traditional training programs.

After having extensive experience in both manager and leader positions, I realized that the training given in these areas was devoid of sufficient practical tips for helping me to operate successfully in the positions given me. Although the several institutions I attended gave me the theoretical frameworks for managing and leading, I was left without a mental grounding for explaining these and for helping myself and others move onward and upward in these two closely related arenas. This concerned me greatly because most individuals are required to play management and leadership roles of some type from time to time. I reasoned that if these were given plausible definitions for the terms, concrete ideas of what is expected of the people involved in these practices, and tips and strategies for being effective and for evaluating their own and their organization's effectiveness, they would not only be able to fit in the workplace better, but also be more prepared to be successful in setting ourselves apart as strong managers and leaders.

This chapter, stemming from the research and study conducted to improve my own abilities, is intended to help arm those who aspire to be really good managers and leaders. Its focus is to clarify both roles, show how both arenas are entwined, and give them tips and strategies for playing their roles more effectively. In realizing that even a short study on effective management and leadership that is devoid of lessons on *planning* and *organizing* cannot be called complete, I have devoted the two chapters that follow to these topics. I feel that both topics deserve separate chapters due to their being the two most comprehensive and most utilized of the principles developed for managers, but that are also used extensively by effective leaders.

The topics covered within the 3 sections of this chapter are seen as essential for those wishing to have an edge in fulfilling their managing and leading roles. These sections are described below:

Section A is devoted to the management basics. While It is thought that because their work is mainly conducted in an office environment, and their responsibilities do not include having to train others, most managers are usually not called leaders in the absolute sense. Still, as the head of their offices, they have leadership responsibilities; therefore, having a sound basic grounding concerning the leadership component involved, is essential for dealing with the practical side of management.

Section B is devoted to leadership. While many say that "leading" is a calling, all agree that it must be honed through study and practice. It is felt that when the basic leadership topics covered in this section are included in the arsenals of knowledge of success-oriented individuals, they will be more effective in separating themselves from others in the practice of this allimportant art.

Section C, entitled "Management and Leadership In A Nutshell" is devoted to providing insights for comparing and contrasting the two professions, and to showing how both professions are entwined in actual practice.

<h1>SECTION A</h1>

<h1>MANAGEMENT</h1>

Putting the management function in a nutshell

Two items have been selected for this section:

In <u>An Overview of Management</u>, a method is shown for forming a practical definition for the terms *"management"* and *"a manager."* In addition, the resources that managers control are identified, and the principles that guide the management act are listed.

In <u>The Basic Organizational Model</u>, a description is given of the three levels of management that exist within almost all organizations. In that this model may be used to represent the family construct, businesses, governments, and institutions, it is applicable in a true universal sense. When individuals take care to understand where they fit within a specific portion of the model representing the entity they are participating in, and when they commit to meeting the expectations incumbent on them at that level, they can hardly be held back from being successful.

An Overview of Management

In providing an overview of management it is best to begin with defining the terms *management* and *a manager*. This is because the definitions found in the dictionary are not complete enough for individuals to grasp what practical management really means, and what managers are principally concerned about. The definitions below are intended to expand on those provided in the dictionary:

Management is the act or process utilized by a person or persons to control an organization's resources that include: 1) personnel, 2) the budget, 3) facilities, 4) equipment, 4) materials, 5) supplies, and 6) time.

A *manager* is a person who is concerned with controlling the resources of a business, team, organization, or enterprise.

In small organizations managers with only one or two assistants are judged by their superiors in terms of efficiency displayed in handling the resources given them to manage, with the emphasis being on the people under their control and budgetary matters. In larger organizations, managers may have assistants responsible for controlling one or more of the entity's resources. In either case, managers may expect to be evaluated on both their and their employees' knowledge, skills, and performances as they pertain to the principles developed for dealing with organizational resources.

Management Principles. The principles of management also serve as the principles of administration. While a good understanding of each principle is a prerequisite for all who wish to be regarded as professional managers and administrators, being able to apply them skillfully should be the aim of all with such a quest. While it is thought that having simplistic definitions for each of the 5 principles as shown below will provide an edge for practitioners in these fields, it follows that practitioners will strive to learn as much as possible concerning each of them.

1. Planning—to form a scheme or program for the accomplishment or attainment of.

2. Organizing—to put together into an orderly, functional structured whole.

3. Directing—to give authoritative instructions to.

4. Coordinating—to form a pleasing combination in order to harmonize actions and efforts in a common cause.

5. Controlling—to exercise authoritative or dominating influence over using an instrument or set of instruments to guide the actions of.

The Basic Organizational Model

The scope of managerial enterprise is undertaken within the framework of a three-tiered organizational model where the 5 principles of management—planning, organizing, directing, coordinating, and controlling—are brought to bear. It follows that having a general understanding of how these principles are applied within this framework gives the ordinary person a knowledge edge when called on to perform management and leadership duties. For those who wish to be defined as excellent managers and leaders, it is imperative that they have practical skills for employing these principles in an organizational setting.

While information concerning the employment of the principles of management runs throughout this and the next two chapters, I believe that all, including practitioners, should have at ready a mental picture of the typical organizational setting. For this reason, I have identified the threetiered level that exists within normal organizations, and have devised a simple model for describing the primary function of individuals located within each level. These are shown below:

The 3 Levels Within a Typical Organization

- The top level where those providing top management and support are located.

- The level above the base where the organizational leader and his staff are located.

- The bottom level where base level workers are located.

The Primary Functions of Individuals Participating Within the 3 Organizational Levels

The Upper Level – Individuals located at this level are the major stakeholders. Their responsibilities include: providing governing policies, developing organizational aims and objectives, providing logistical and other support, conducting formal inspections, and receiving and acting on reports from the managers and leaders of major sub-organizations..

The Middle Level – Individuals within this level consist of the sub-unit manager and his assistants and staff members. This manager is the all-knowing problem-solver who keeps the objectives of the upper level administrators in mind, and is not a stranger to the basic workplace. The assistants and staff members are responsible for: 1) advising the manager, 2) developing and implementing administrative and operational policy, and 3) for assisting the organizational leader in all aspects of planning, organizing, directing, coordinating, and controlling the unit's resources of time, personnel, finances, property, equipment, facilities, and supplies. Additionally, these operatives supervise and evaluate the sub-units' performances, and maintain administrative, training, and other records that pertain to the organization at large.

The Base Level – Teams and workers within the sub-organizations are located at this level. These operate generally in a team-working environment, with responsibilities for knowing their jobs, obeying all orders and directives, and performing all tasks assigned in accordance with organizational procedures.

SECTION B

LEADERSHIP

Improving your leadership potential

Four items have been selected for this section:

In <u>An Overview of Leadership</u>, a method is shown for forming a practical definition for the terms *"leadership"* and *"a leader."* In addition, an explanation of leader requirements are given; the four major principles that all who wish to be expert leaders should apply are listed; the aspect of leadership effectiveness is touched on; and examples of four of the leadership principles in action are presented.

In <u>Leadership Traits</u>, the character traits that identify good leaders are listed and explained.

In <u>The Indicators of Leadership</u>, four unique indicators, or pointers to leadership effectiveness, are highlighted. These allow the quality of leadership being displayed in an organization to be determined, and they serve to identify the aspects of leadership needing special attention.

In <u>A Leadership Scenario</u>, a situation is highlighted to emphasize the impact and importance of the indicators of leadership, and how they play in to sparking decisions and initiatives that impact on organizational improvement.

An Overview Of Leadership

While being at the head of an organization may be seen by some as leading it, unless the person in this position is involved with the requirements real leaders are judged on, it is probably best to call such a male person "the point man." Instances of this variety of leading is displayed when the point man is not necessarily the leader, as can be seen in the game "Follow the Leader," and when a player or another individual is designated to lead a football team onto the field. As there is no redeeming value in following lead persons in this fashion, individuals who wish to be regarded as real leaders need to be armed with a basic understanding of the terms, *leadership* and *a leader*. In that being able to define thee two terms is basic to being conversant in conversations pertinent to the art of leadership, my simplistic definitions are provided below:

Leadership is the process of influencing people by providing them with the purpose, direction, and motivation to accomplish tasks assigned, while sponsoring activities that impact on skill development and organizational improvement.

A leader is one with the ability to influence others to complete a task properly and on time.

What Leaders Provide

- Purpose: The reason to act in order to achieve a desired end.

- Direction: Communicating how to accomplish the task.

- Motivation: Supplying the will to do what is necessary to accomplish the task.

Interestingly enough, the definitions cited above can be utilized as the basis for not only selecting individuals for leadership positions, but also as guidelines for Individuals to follow who are serving in these positions. When selected for leadership, wise individuals commit to applying the principles established to guide their own activities, and to making organizational members more successful.

Four Key Leadership Principles

As for the principles of leadership, there are several; however, the four that are extremely important are:

1. Know yourself and seek improvement.
2. Set the example.
3. Know your subordinates and look out for their welfare.
4. Train your subordinates as a team.

The Basis For Being Effective

Although the four key principles already mentioned take center-stage in the effectiveness arena, there are several more guiding principles that leaders may refer to in assessing their effectiveness. Among these are:

- *seek responsibility;*

- *be technically and tactically proficient;*

- *make sound and timely decisions;*

- *keep subordinates informed,*

- *develop a sense of responsibility in them;* and

- *employ the unit in accordance with its capabilities.*

Although all are important, I feel that when the four already listed are employed in a steadfast manner, the base requirement for being truly effective will be met. In my view, because these four principles serve to give a concrete idea of what is universally expected of leaders, and because they deal explicitly with the leader and his relationship with subordinate, they serve as absolute effectiveness guides for leaders of all kinds in building up their teams and improving their organizations.

Notes on the Leadership Principles

- *Know yourself and seek improvement*: Leaders must be aware of their own strengths and weaknesses, and must commit to eliminating their weaknesses and improving on their strengths.

- *Set the example*: Leaders must hold themselves in such a way that they serve as models representing the pattern of behavior that distinguishes their team or group.

- *Know your subordinates and look out for their welfare*: Leaders must take steps to become better acquainted with their subordinates. This includes having knowledge of their *strongest points*—those that can be utilized in improving the organization; as well as their *weakest points*—those requiring special attention in order for unit effectiveness to be upgraded. When one is looking out for the welfare of team members, it is necessary to see that all are treated fairly, fully supported, and provided incentives that promote proficiency, discipline, high morale, and a spirit of teamwork.

- *Train your subordinates as a team*: Leaders train team members with the objective of having them work together smoothly in accomplishing tasks can be in a timely fashion, and with all assigned carrying their fair share of the load.

Although these four key principles take center stage in the effectiveness arena, leaders can refer to the following guides in assessing their own effectiveness:

- Seek responsibility
- Be technically and tactically proficient
- Make sound and timely decisions
- Keep subordinates informed
- Develop a sense of responsibility in subordinates
- Employ the unit in accordance with its capabilities.

Notes on Leader and Subordinate Responsibilities

- <u>Team leaders</u>, like organizational leaders, are responsible for the training, discipline, and employment of their teams. It should be noted that "discipline," usually associated with *punishment,* is not punishment in this sense. While the purpose of most punishment is to give an individual an opportunity to rehabilitate himself or herself, the purpose of discipline is to instill a culture of teamwork, wherein team members automatically follow uniform procedures in accomplishing assigned tasks, and in readying themselves to meet evaluation criteria.

- <u>Assistant team leaders</u> are responsible for assisting the team leader in the discipline, training, and employment of the team.

- <u>Other team members</u> are responsible for obeying all instructions, and for doing their best at all times.

Leadership Traits

Definition of Trait: A distinguishing feature, as of a person's character.

Although the list of general character traits is long, the fourteen character traits listed below have been identified for years in military officers' training programs as important for displaying effective leadership. In that each of these represents an admirable personal quality, successoriented individuals who also wish to have the admiration of their peers and gain real solid reputations, will do well to add this list to other personal traits that define them, such as: being kind, thoughtful, caring, etc. While the notes following each trait listed below are intended to help in understanding what is meant by the term, they also serve as guides for those who aspire to leadership positions, and who wish to build upon their reputations as leaders and team players.

1. **B**EARING (*Taking care to be considerate of how one looks and acts.*)
2. **C**OURAGE (*Displaying both physical and moral courage. Physical courage is the quality that enables one to resolutely face danger and fear; moral courage is displayed by a willingness to stand up for, say, or do what is right.*)
3. **D**EPENDABILITY (*Being counted on to be in the right place on time; for keeping one's word; and for doing what is expected.*)
4. **D**ECISIVENESS (*Making sound and timely decisions.*)
5. **E**NTHUSIASM (*Approaching tasks with vigor and with a positive attitude.*)
6. **E**NDURANCE (*Being willing to endure, to complete the race.*)
7. **I**NITIATIVE (*Taking proper steps without waiting to be told.*)
8. **I**NTEGRITY (*Being honest; keeping to a strict ethical code.*)
9. **J**UDGMENT (*Thinking first, before acting.*)
10. **J**USTICE (*Being fair; impartial.*)
11. **K**NOWLEDGE (*Showing understanding on the basis of experience and study.*)
12. **L**OYALTY (*Being true to others, and to a cause or organization.*)
13. **S**ELFLESSNESS (*Not allowing actions to be self-centered; thinking of others first.*)
14. **T**ACT (*Saying and doing that which will not offend others.*)

The Indicators Of Leadership

Paying attention to four "indicators" is key to the success of an organizational leader

Proficiency – Discipline – Morale – Organizational Pride

The four terms listed above are utilized universally to assess the status of leadership effectiveness within an organization. These, aptly called *The Indicators of Leadership,* are of great value to supervisors within institutions established to develop products or to produce skills. While they are also useful in evaluating an organization, they also have great value in making judgments concerning what aspects of leadership within an organization are in need of repair, as well as in foretelling how well a unit is prepared to accomplish its assigned missions. As each of the indicators can be referred to during the evaluation of a subordinate leader's performance, supervisors use them extensively in describing the unique aspects of both individual and unit performances..

While the indicators are useful to individuals wishing to determine early if the position they are interested in is within a poorly led or a well led organization, it is important to note that leaders at every level may use the indicators to determine if they are leading satisfactorily, or if improvements in their methods are necessary. It follows, therefore, that individuals who aspire to better themselves should not only be thoroughly familiar with the role the indicators play in assessing a leadership situation, but also with how they can be brought to bear on their own efforts and on organizational success.

As a tip for recalling the four indicators upon which leadership performances will be judged, the letters **PDMO** are useful as a memory cue.

Proficiency is best determined by evaluating the individual skills of the leader, as well as the knowledge and skills displayed by the members of the unit or team. Knowing this, wise leaders take pains to insure an equitable plan for building up the skills of organizational members is in place.

While formal evaluations concerning proficiency are conducted by the leadership at higher organizational levels on an annual or semi-annual basis, these evaluations are usually in the form of questions. Wise leaders, upon perusing the entire list of questions, assume responsibility for responding positively to those that fall in the areas that pertain to their individual roles and to the organization as a whole. After giving responsibility to their subleaders for responding positively to the questions that pertain to their roles, they establish schedules for testing and determining the proficiency levels of all within the organization using the same criteria as that utilized by the higher authority. It goes without saying that very wise leaders follow-up with schedules for taking corrective action, and with follow-up evaluations in order to insure their organizations meet or exceed expectations.

In that proficiency evaluation results give leaders input regarding their subordinates value to the organization as well as well as their potential for upward mobility, wise leaders take pains to insure that those who meet the criteria established for special training and schooling are given opportunities for such on an equitable basis.

Discipline within an organization is best determined by evaluating how well the standardized procedures within an organization are being followed. When these procedures have been developed to insure the fail-safeness of organizational activities, they are made a part of individual and team job descriptions. In well-disciplined units such procedures, called SOP's, are tested on a periodic basis in order to insure that the organization policy is being followed and that its units are functioning in such a way that only minor corrections, if any, are needed to meet or exceed expectations.

Discipline within organizations is heightened when the members are informed of the fact that the high standards achieved during operations and evaluations are the result of the unit having well-oiled procedures to follow. It is heightened also when unit members are told that the organization has set itself apart from sister units that are not guided by such standard operating procedures.

Morale pertains to all things within an organization that have to do with the well being of the individuals involved, to include feeding plans, mail, pay, family concerns, etc. This is why wise leaders institute an open-door policy for entertaining discussions that deal with these aspects and other morale issues. When problems are brought to the leader's attention he takes steps to insure that corrective action plans are implemented immediately to resolve these and issues related to them.

When organizational members are aware of the fact that their welfare is a primary concern of the leadership arm, these members will go out of their way in compensating for this concern.

Organization Pride, called esprit de corps in the military, is a term used in describing the degree (high, low, unsatisfactory) of pride unit members have in being part of the organization. Wise leaders do not fail in recognizing and making individual and unit contributions and achievements known, and in describing the path the organization is taking in order to become even better.

When leaders stake pains to inform unit members of the positive impressions the unit has made on higher echelon leaders, and to make note of their responses to member concerns brought to their attention, not only will organizational pride be heightened, so too will member willingness to work even harder to maintain and exceed organizational expectations.

When all four of the indicators are in tact, the expectation is that the leader will have no trouble meeting requirements, and that the organization will not fail in accomplishing all goals assigned. It should be noted, however, that when more than one of these indicators is wanting, the leader will be challenged to fully meet the expectations of his office, and it can be expected that the organization will be a troubled one.

A Leadership Scenario

The purpose of the following scenario is to highlight the value of indicators of leadership in making decisions regarding organizational activities that need to be standardized and regimented.

Scenario

Part 1. A new district superintendent, who decided to visit one of her award-winning schools in athletics, telephoned the school to announce her intended visit. At this time she made note of the fact that the person taking the call did not give a formal greeting when answering. Later, during her visit and while taking a tour of the school dining facility, she noticed that the mops outside the facility were dirty and that the dishwashing machine had not been cleaned properly. Her visit to one classroom gave her some concerns in that the substitute teacher had not been given a lesson plan to follow, and the students were playing games on her with respect to classmates who were absentees. She noticed also that a few students were in the hallway talking outside two other classrooms, and that the students in those classrooms had not been given learning objectives for the subject being presented. During her meeting with the student body and faculty in the auditorium she observed that it took an overlong period for the principal to quiet the students so that the program could begin, and was disappointed in seeing that the members of the faculty were grouped at the very back of the assembly hall.

Part 2. After mulling over the situation at the school, the superintendent drew the conclusion that the leadership at the school was failing, and that this was an indication that her other schools may also be in need of her help. She decided to take action by discussing her observations during a meeting with all her principals and issuing the following edict in writing:

All district schools are directed to review the manner in which their daily activities are conducted, and establish standard procedures (SOP's) for routine operations that include the following:

1. The official greeting to be used by office personnel when taking telephone calls.
2. The care and cleaning of the kitchen and equipment items.
3. A classroom management standard that includes lesson plans, student seating plans, and classroom conduct and attendance protocol.
4. A procedure for beginning class sessions; to include a special provision for the announcement of student learning objectives.
5. The protocol for faculty member intervention in student group settings, including those in the assembly hall and at fire drills and pep rallies.

School SOP's covering these items, to include how items 3, 4, and 5 above will be adapted in a substitute teacher regimen, are to be delivered to me by each school principal NLT 15 days after receipt of this missive.

_____

Superintendent of Schools

SECTION C

A PRACTICAL VIEW
OF MANAGEMENT
AND LEADERSHIP

Anyone can dig a ditch, but not everyone can tell you how.

While books on the subjects of management and leadership are usually produced as separate entities extolling theories and examples of their applications in various fields of practice, they rarely point to the interrelatedness of the two art forms. In my view, this interrelatedness should be highlighted. I believe that when the differences and similarities between the two are clarified, the commonality of the functions incumbent on both good managers and leaders will become clearer. As a start in developing a practical view of these important art forms, it is best to refer to the definitions arrived at in the earlier sections:

Management: The act or process utilized by a person or persons to control an organization's resources that include: people, budgets, facilities. equipment, materials, supplies, and time.

A manager is a person who is concerned with controlling the resources of a business, team, organization, or enterprise.

81

<u>Leadership</u>: The process of influencing people by providing purpose, direction, and motivation, in order to accomplish assigned tasks and to improve the organization.

<u>A leader</u> is one with the ability to influence others to complete a task properly and on time.

The four definitions above are intended to be useful in showing that both are process activated, and that the main concern of one practice is in handling people and a number of other resources, and that the other's main concern in handling with only one resource – people. As this is the focus of this section, I have selected one piece from my success program in order to highlight the manner ion which I view both practices. The purpose of the discussion entitled "Management And Leadership In A Nutshell" is to add to the overviews given on these topics in earlier portions of this chapter, and to provide the pictures individuals who wish to have an advantage on their contemporaries need to emplace in their portfolios of knowledge.

The first viewpoint put forth explains the reason why individuals are designated as managers or leaders and gives an overview of how these are entwined in actual practice. The next viewpoints address the major differences and similarities in the lore developed to describe the practices of both managing and leading. The entire discussion is intended to show that while the art of managing and the art of leading are grounded in separate fields, those who wish define themselves as really good managers and leaders must consign themselves to wearing a hat, so to speak, that represents both fields of expertise. They must not only have an understanding of the essential skills that are usually identified in the practice of the other's field of work, but must also be able to demonstrate competency in utilizing these skills as expertly as possible in the practice of their own field of work.

Management And Leadership In A Nutshell

Core thoughts for understanding both concepts

<u>Clarifying The Need For Managers and Leaders</u>

-- "There would be no need for managers unless they are required to control or direct people and other resources of an organization in accordance with principles or values that have already been established."

-- "There would be no need for leaders unless they are utilized to train, regulate, and employ the members of their organizations in accomplishing tasks for which the unit was developed."

From the above statements, it can be readily understood that individuals are called managers and leaders because they have different functional roles. It can be deduced from these that most managers operate usually from static positions and have responsibilities that deal mainly with one or a set of organizational resources. This is why organizations break down portions of their enterprise into parts wherein a specific entity or a specified number of resources are provided a designated manager to control or direct. As examples, some organizations elect to have office managers, budget managers, managers of facilities, and managers of research and development. Conversely, it can also be deduced that most leaders do not normally operate from static positions due to the responsibilities incumbent on them for training and deploying unit members.

A View of Management and Leadership in Practice

Because of the interrelatedness of management and leadership, it behooves those who wish to rise above what is seen as just a good operator in the field of management or that of leadership, to learn as much as possible about the primary workings of managers and leaders, and how these workings are entwined in the practice of individuals holding these positions.

The manager, in controlling an organization's resources, understands that the most important resources he must manage are the people within the organization and the budgets of concern. He must be fully cognizant of what is expected of him, what preparation and study is necessary to do his job, what relationships he is establish or maintain, and the manner in which he and his unit are to be evaluated. In order to be identified as an excellent performer, he must strive to show himself also as an effective leader. This is done by: having a general understanding of leadership and the expectations of leaders, being consistent in displaying certain behavioral characteristics, using the indicators which denote leadership effectiveness, and by applying the principles that guide the profession of leaders as imperatives also for being successful in the managerial arena.

In a similar vein, the leader, who is mainly concerned with the accomplishment of missions and with organizational improvement, must be cognizant of the requirements of the position, his own and his organization's strengths and weaknesses, the relationships he is to build upon, and the process that will be utilized in evaluating both his and his organization's performance. In order to be identified as an excellent performer, he must not only display knowledge, skills, and characteristics that define him as a crafty practitioner in influencing others to be successful, he must strive to be an adept manager. This is done by having a general understanding of management and the major expectations of managers, and by honing the managerial skills that are imperative in fully carrying out his leadership responsibilities.

Success in the performance arena is assured for manager-leaders and leader-managers if they plan for, organize, and develop their unit members to perform as a team, standardize routine procedures, and prepare themselves and their subordinates for programmed evaluations. This, the latter, is done by being aware of written and stated evaluation criteria, and by taking appropriate steps to meet or exceed the expectations of evaluators.

Managing and Leading

As implied earlier, since most training courses pertinent to a field of work emphasize theories, and not aspects pertaining to the practice of the art involved, the individuals completing these courses are unable to speak with clarity concerning the nature of work in their particular field, nor of the fundamentals and principles that guide their performances. While this is probably due to the fact that books guiding the coursework are developed by authors who are not managers, and to the fact that the instructors usually have little professional management experience. Although professional managers are sometimes brought in as instructors, it is likely that their presentations do not leave students with ready responses for defining or for describing the art of management, and their lessons do not always connect the need for managers to exercise useful attributes borrowed from the leadership arena.

In not connecting the leadership component with the manager's responsibilities, these instructors too often leave their students with vague ideas concerning the practice of management. In view of this reality, it should come as no surprise that their students are not provided with mental formats for dealing with the principles under-girding the management functions of planning, organizing, directing, coordinating, and controlling. While this is the seat of the trouble, it is not resolved in the workplace. It may be assumed that the bosses located in the workplace are not well grounded in both these important fields.

It follows that in addition to committing themselves to learning as much as possible about how planning, organizing, directing, coordinating, and controlling organizational resources, aspirants interested in climbing higher in the arena of management should commit to learning as much as possible about leadership and how it is entwined in playing their management roles. As this entwinement is of utmost importance, those who wish to be defined as expert managers should have plausible answers to address the following questions:

- Do I have practical definitions for management and manager, as well as for leadership, leader?

- Are there certain personal characteristics I can display that define me as a managerleader?

- Is there a set of principles I can adopt that will help me in being more effective as a manager-leader?

- Are there certain styles available to me that will be useful in my being more effective?

- Is there something I can do to improve the competences of those I manage?

- Is there a set of indicators I can turn to that will allow me to determine my own and my organization's effectiveness?

- What communications measures can I put in place to insure my people are well informed and that organizational control is not lost?

Leading and Managing

As with management, the books that guide potential leaders in training courses are written by authors who may be scholars, but hardly ever by persons who are steeped in the practice of leading. While the books utilized do a rather good job of both defining leadership and identifying the principles that apply to good leader performances, the instructors, devoid of management experience, are unable to connect the art of leadership with good management practices. As a result, the instruction flags in giving students ready and plausible answers to questions pertinent to defining their leader and manager roles, and for explaining the practical aspects of the leadership and its connection with managing effectively.

As a result, too many leaders cannot readily respond to questions regarding: their roles, how these roles will be assessed, how to size up their units, how the styles of leadership can be utilized for fulfilling both leader and manager duties, and how the, principles established to guide their performances are appropriate in dealing with their leader and manager concerns. When so armed with these responses, those who aspire to be good leaders will have an edge on their less informed contemporaries.

With these as start points, the following is offered for connecting the key aspects of leadership in playing the leader-manager's role with skill:

- The main function of leader-managers is to *serve*. They serve those in the chain above them and they serve those they lead.

- Leader-managers must be aware that they are evaluated on the skills they display in carrying out their primary responsibilities of training, instilling discipline, and in readying organizational members to undertake leadership and management tasks that may be assigned.

- In sizing up their units, leader-managers know:

    -- That their unit is proficient when its members perform their duties with skill.

-- That their unit is well disciplined when its members can be relied on to be where they are supposed to be, and doing what they are supposed to be doing without always being told.

-- That high morale is the expectation when the essentials having to do with the well being of its members are in place.

-- That their unit is a prideful one when its members maintain high performance standards, and relish the unit's position among its competitors.

There are several styles of leadership; however, the most popular utilized by leader-managers are:

- The Directing Style. Used when time is of essence and subordinates have not been well trained.

- The Delegating Style. Used when subordinate leaders are proficient enough for responsibility and authority to be given them to lead others.

- The Participating Style. Used when the leader needs to be in the mix of activity, or when the leader is sizing up his organization's proficiency in accomplishing tasks.

In addition to displaying proper traits of character, keeping their personnel well informed, and making good decisions regarding organizational procedures, leader-managers are able to distinguish themselves when they have plausible answers for addressing the following questions:

- Do I have practical definitions for *leadership, a leader,* and for *management,* as well as for *a manager*?

- Are there certain personal characteristics I can display that define me as a good leader- manager?

- Is there a set of principles I can adopt that will help me in being more effective as a leader-manager?

- Are there other styles available that will be useful in my being more effective?

- Is there something I can do to improve the competences of those I lead?

- Is there a set of indicators I can turn to that will allow me to determine my own and my organization's effectiveness?

- What communications measures can I put in place to insure my people are well informed and that organizational control is not lost?

CHAPTER VIII

ON PLANNING FOR YOUR SUCCESS

The hallmark of all successful operations is sound and complete planning

The concept of planning is considered by many as the first and foremost of the principles of management and administration due to the integral part it plays in dealing with its sister principles. Others say that it is just the first of the principles, and that organizing is just as important because of its connection with each of the other principles. While I do not take a position as to which of the two is predominant, I believe that tips concerning both far-reaching principles should be passed on to the success-oriented in separate chapters.

In this chapter the position I take is that in developing a sound planning scheme, a set of basic questions serve as pillars of thought. These questions are as follows:

1. What do I want to accomplish?
2. What ways are open to me to get to this point?
3. Who or what is needed to support this effort?
4. What decisions do I need to make concerning the above in order to complete my plan?

While the questions above apply to simple planning projects, reasoned responses to them is deemed to be the first on the list of planning considerations for projects of all kinds. This is because these help in clarifying the planner's intent, identifying the choices open to be analyzed, and in determining the best manner in which others and their resources are to be involved.

For complex planning projects, responses to another set of questions serve as pillars of thought for organizational planners, and as assists to planners within supporting units and organizations. These questions are as follows:

1. How much planning time is available?
2. What opposition is anticipated?
3. What movement and storage will be required?
4. What facilities are available?
5. What coordination measures are necessary?
6. What communication scheme is best for developing and executing this plan?
7. Who will control the operation and from what location(s)?

While it is clear that planning on a sophisticated level will not be a priority issue until weddings, banquets, conventions, etc., have to be planned for, I am convinced that understanding the art and science of planning as promulgated in my success program is a must for managers, leaders, and success-oriented individuals. The 3 topics below have been selected for this chapter in order to promote this understanding:

- Planning Act Considerations
- Simple and Complex Planning
- Developing A Plan For Recurring Activities—The SOP

Planning Act Considerations

Planning is a necessity for a variety of administrative and tactical uses. As examples, it is common for organizations to have safety plans, fire escape plans, financial plans, investment plans, fund-raising plans, retirement plans, etc. Regardless of whether a plan is to be used administratively or tactically, the main point to be kept in mind is that those involved in the undertaking should also be involved when possible in the decision-making and problem-solving aspects of the plan. It should also be kept in mind that conserving the resources of time, people, money, facilities, supplies, equipment, and materials of the base organization as well as of supporting elements is of vital importance.

How Decisions Become Plans in Organizations

In large organizations the planning process begins when the leader provides staff planners with an early statement concerning his intent. Staff planners, in insuring that the key elements identified for study and analysis are considered, utilize the established planning format developed within their organizations, and planners continue the process by proposing recommendations based on decisions designed to reach the objective established as quickly and as safely as possible with the least expenditure of organizational resources. When these recommendations, subject to be changed as a result of the leader's interventions, are approved, a final plan is issued to subordinate leaders to be carried out.

In most cases, plans are developed for implementation within a timing scheme where the start time is one of the most important elements. In such cases, the leader's intent is to have his staff develop plans so that an operation *begins* at a certain time. While this technique is called *forward planning*, in the case of an airborne operation where the intent to have paratroopers arrive on a landing zone at a certain time before an operation begins, *backward planning*—wherein the time of flight must be factored in—is the first requirement. In the case of a fundraising campaign, plans are made to deal with the front, middle, and end portions of the program.

All this is to say that regardless of the planning scheme, individuals who understand the base level considerations for complete planning, will have an advantage over their contemporaries who have not been fully introduced to these considerations.

Base Level Considerations for Complete Planning

<u>The Mission</u> & <u>The Leader's Intent</u>

<u>The Situation</u> & <u>The Task Assigned</u>

<u>The Courses of Action Available</u>

<u>Analyses of The Courses of Action</u> & <u>A Timing Scheme for Action</u>

<u>The Support Scheme</u> & <u>The Logistics Involved</u>

<u>Miscellaneous Considerations</u>

The annotations below are intended to clarify the 12 base level considerations listed above. When these considerations have been made, they are entered in *The 7-Part Format For Complete Planning*.

Understanding Base Level Considerations

- **The Mission**: A clear statement of the main objective or the objectives assigned the organization.

- **The Leader's Intent**: Prior to the initiation of the planning act in formal organizations, the leader informs his staff planners of his initial thoughts, to include his major concerns. At this time he gives guidance for dealing with his immediate concerns, and sets time deadlines for receiving staff recommendations and for the completion of planning activities.

- **The Situation**: A primary consideration in all planning activities is a thorough examination of the current situation (what has been happening and what is happening at the moment?), and the anticipated situation (what will probably be the case when the plan is implemented?).

- **The Statement of the Task**: In developing the task statement denoting the assignment of objectives, planners are careful to include additional tasks that have been implied in the original mission statement.

- **The Courses of Action Available**: In almost all cases there will be at least two or three ways in which task accomplishment can be approached. The <u>direct approach</u> is taken when time is of essence; however, <u>less direct approaches</u> are considered when safety and security become a major issue with the more direct approach. When it is deemed that certain intermediate objectives should be avoided altogether because facing them head-on or even indirectly will be a resource-consuming task, the <u>by-pass approach</u> becomes a consideration.

- **Analysis of the Courses of Action (C/A)**: In recommending a main course of action, planners, base their decisions on their analyses of the advantages and disadvantages of each C/A under consideration. In analyzing each C/A, planners consider their own strengths and weaknesses, the opportunities availed by the situation, and the threats envisioned that may challenge the operation (These are called SWOT Analyses).

  Because the main C/A selected will be chosen on the basis of which one will best accomplish the leader's intent, a comparative analysis is carefully conducted of all C/A selected. In weighing the advantages and disadvantages of the C/A available, the elements given primary consideration are safety and security during movement, the location and importance of intermediate objectives, and the wisest utilization of organizational and support resources in reaching the main objective. The decision points in these analyses are mostly concerned with (1) which C/A is considered best on the basis of speed, and (2) which C/A is more advantageous to the organization on the basis of conserving its resources.

- **A Timing Scheme for Action**: Because timing considerations are of utmost importance in the planning arena, planners are careful to include a timing scheme for activities that take place before, during, and at the end of a contemplated tasking. If, for example, a plan developed by organizational planners is to be further developed and acted on by supporting and subordinate elements, each of these entities must be given its mission as early as possible so it can complete planning and readiness activities within the time frames established.

  In large organizations, the guideline is for the higher unit to estimate the time between receipt of a plan and start of the operation, and, thereafter, to utilize no more than one-third of the time for preliminary planning, while allowing two-thirds of this time for subordinate unit planning. When time is of essence, the major planning unit may find it necessary to issue quick, incomplete plans early on (these are called warning orders in the military and in some corporations). Warning orders are issued so that subordinate elements can begin planning or moving to assembly points or to start positions before receiving the final plans being developed.

- **The Support Scheme**: There must be a *scheme of support* for every tactical plan of action involving movement of organizational players. Supporting individuals or organizations must be given their roles in sufficient time to implement their own planning activities. As with the primary leader, the support leader in most formal organizations also expresses his major concerns (leaders intent) to staff planners before their formal planning is initiated.

- **The Logistics Involved**: In all planning situations, the utilization of equipment and materials needed in support of an operational scheme must be carefully considered and made a vital part of the planning effort. In cases where logistics items must be stockpiled to support an operation, the routes, methods, locations, and times of delivery of these items are usually included in the support plans that accompany the operational plans of the major organization.

- **Coordination measures**: In order to eliminate incidents and confusion when organizations move, pass through, or come in close contact with another, coordination measures are planned for. When necessary, liaison personnel fully cognizant of the plans are designated to insure that all entities involved are provided with vital information, to include: communication codes, locations, contact times, and the identification of counterpart contact agents.

- **A System of Communication**: A communications system whereby leaders of both the operational and support entities can be reached directly for coordination and control is imperative in all planning situations. A variety of communications methods may be a part of the overall communications scheme; however, care must be taken to insure that all communications, along with emergency contact measures, are tested and kept operational.

- **Miscellaneous Considerations**: It is imperative that leaders and organizational planners consider the impact of weather and travel conditions, and give thought to dealing with non-standard activities and with complex issues that impact on mission accomplishment. Non-standard issues may require establishing procedures for dealing with incidents, emergencies, addressing the personal preferences of visiting dignitaries, or non-expected visitors. Other issues, like being called on to brief follow-on plans or to conduct a demonstration, may require planners to arrange for and conduct rehearsals.

Simple And Complex Planning

Because simple and complex planning activities must begin in the minds of all planners, they need a set of thought-provoking questions to ask themselves in both cases. It is thought this technique will lead to the development of more questions and to answers that are important in producing well thought out and failsafe tactics and strategies. While the following lists of questions are intended to promote the kind of thinking considered essential to the start of wise planning, the statement following the sets of questions posed below may be seen as a key action tip for those who aspire to be successful planners.

Questions For Simple Planning

1. What must be done and by what time?
2. What situations and problems are involved?
3. Who is available to help?
4. How many ways can the task be accomplished?
5. Which of the several ways will produce the most satisfactory results?

Action Tip: Choose the best of these ways; develop a plan for action; insure that all involved are aware of the problem to be resolved or the objective to be reached; and designate the part they are expected to play.

Questions For Complex Planning

1. What are the tasks, and what is the leader's intent?
2. What is the situation now, and how is it expected to change?
3. What courses of action are available?
4. Which course of action offers the best advantage?
5. Who is supporting, and with what resources?
6. What are the timing considerations that bear on planning and on the execution of the plan? [It may be necessary to issue a tentative plan to facilitate the planning of subordinate units prior to completing the final plan.]
7. What coordination measures should be planned for? [The key is to consider probable adverse situations and controls necessary for eliminating confusion]

8. What logistics are involved (gasoline, equipment, food, water, supplies, etc.)? [The key is to have adequate provisions for storage, distribution, and a sound program for replacing all items in the logistics chain, to include personnel.]

9. What communication measures must be implemented? [The key is to have multiple means of communicating, and the capability to keep these means and their backup systems up and running.]

10. Where will the leader be located? [In case communications fail, sub-leaders need to know how to reach the physical locations of their leaders in order to report the status of operations, and to inform them of problems that bear on unit success.]

11. Have procedures been established to deal with non-standard activities, and have needed rehearsals been arranged for and scheduled,?

Action Tip: Arrange a meeting of key players in order to present the complete plan, answer questions, and resolve issues that impact negatively on operational readiness.

The 7-Part Format For Complete Planning

- Mission (What is the requirement? When will it begin?)

- Situation (What is happening? What will be happening when this operation begins? What impact will opposing forces have on our operation?)

- Execution (What action is contemplated? What elements will be involved, and what decisive roles will these play in reaching the objective?)

- Coordinating Instructions (What information is needed so that counterpart elements understand the specific roles assigned the other, and that will eliminate confusion between participating elements?)

- Support Considerations (What elements will provide support and what logistic considerations must be allowed for?)

- Communications (What will be the primary and alternate means for passing on information and receiving reports?)

- Control (What element is responsible for managing and supervising the operation, and from what location(s)?

Developing Plans For Recurring Activities – The Sop

The SOP, an acronym for *Standard Operating Procedures*, is a document dictating a set of explicit instructions established for the uniform handling of tasks or events that organizations and individuals must deal with on a daily or periodic basis. It is derived from decisions made regarding the most effective way to save time, effort, and resources.

SOP's in the organizational setting are considered excellent tools in that supervisor input is unnecessary when dealing with routine occurrences; however, this input is necessary when something different from the norm occurs. For example, if a catering company normally loads its supplies and equipment for a picnic on four company trucks, an SOP loading plan, if established for each truck, will facilitate the orderly loading of all items required by drivers or workers without direction or supervision. However, if only 3 trucks are available on the day of a catering project, the supervisor must get involved in order to insure that the important items for starting the project arrive at the picnic site in the first 3 trucks, while one truck can be designated to return to the loading site to pick up the items left behind that were less urgently needed.

Personal SOP's may be developed as written notes regarding an individual's decisions for standardizing certain procedures; however, they may elect to maintain certain of their procedures as mental notes. Some well-organized people will admit to establishing routines for their regular days and for special events that are to be evaluated and scored. Among these are teachers, lawyers, accountants, and others who understand the value of having concrete plans that guard against wasting time, making excuses, and worrying about whether or not they have missed out on preparing to address certain key issues..

Below is an example personal SOP that may be used as a model. It was developed to support a professor who asked for my assistance in motivating a group of college students who needed help with their studies:

Example SOP For A College Student

This SOP, established as a guide for my daily activities, is designed to keep me in a "ready mode" for dealing with my main objective:

> *"To meet or exceed the learning expectations of each class attended, and to show that I have met these expectations when tested."*

A. <u>General</u>. I will develop time, energy, and stress-saving stratagems and devices that will assist me in the gathering of important information, and establish a regimen for being able to retrieve information for further study, and for preparing to be evaluated.

B. <u>My time–saving devices will include</u>:
- A separate loose-leaf notebook for each class, or a notebook that is separated into sections for each class.
- A Notebook Cover Page will be inserted for each course of study that will include basic information about the course, books used, scheduled test dates, and special notes.
- Sufficient copies of a prepared 1st Page for Daily Notes will be on hand to save time and serve to prompt my getting significant information presented during class. This page will include sections for recording: the day's topic, learning objectives, hints concerning special points to be emphasized on exams and quizzes, and assignments.
- An updated 3-4 month calendar for scheduling events of importance.

C. <u>Before Classroom Activities, I will</u>:
- Review earlier notes taken to insure those written hurriedly are made readable and understandable. I will spend as much time as needed to complete the next day's class assignments, and will commit to spend at least 15 minutes on topics within each of my courses every day except Saturdays.
- Conduct most of my studies during daylight hours, and will study no more than 2 hours continually without taking a break.
- Insure that the notes made during study sessions are inserted properly in my notebook(s), and that all books, equipment, and materials needed for my classes are placed in a certain location so that nothing is left behind.
- Set aside a time for relaxing.

- Go to bed, arise in time in to ready myself, tidy up my room, eat breakfast, collect the items I will need during the school day, and leave in sufficient time so as to arrive prior to the beginning of my first class.

D. <u>During Each Class, I will</u>:
- Fill out the important sections of the 1st Page for Daily Notes I have developed, and take key notes on separate pages in the order in which key information is presented.
- Look carefully for *"teacher tells"* that indicate something is to be evaluated, and make note of high points, references, charts, graphs, equations, etc., that should be closely reviewed.
- Make sure that assignments are entered in my notes, and that these and events connected with class requirements are placed on my calendar.

<u>Special Notes</u>:

1. If reading a chapter has been assigned, I will refer to the "Really Reading Concept" where I look to develop one or more test questions concerning the idea on one page, and write answers to these questions developed for further study on another.
2. When dealing with difficult chapters, after listing the topic headings and the major ideas presented therein, I will develop a paragraph in my own words that summarizes and clarifies my understanding of the chapter. In addition, I will develop a list of questions that when answered will add to this understanding.
3. I will also commit myself to practice eating well, resting properly, and exercising daily.

CHAPTER IX

ON ORGANIZING FOR YOUR SUCCESS

"Don't waste time!"

As indicated in the previous chapter, the principle of organizing deserves a chapter of its own due to it being integral to each of other management principles. While it can hardly be denied that most people would be limited if asked to explain the organizing act, I believe this problem can be easily resolved. I am convinced that individuals who are given tips for doing so, and simple organizing skills, they will have fewer problems in getting through their days and handling recurring events. I believe also that they will be even better prepared for handling even larger concerns if they are armed with information and strategies for organizing on even more complex levels.

The information and strategies I have in mind are interred in scenarios from my success program that are intended to help success-oriented individuals in not only being able to speak with clarity about the organizing concept, but also to give them guidelines, formats, and ideas for participating in the organizing act with skill. The 3 scenarios that follow and the discussions that accompany them are designed to serve as short study for dealing with both private and public organizing concerns. The summary at the end is intended to round-out the study.

<u>Scenario A</u>: (Assignment Of A School Support Tasking)

The new instructor for a high school military program received the following note from the school principal:

Colonel,

Please forgive the short notice, but over 200 parents and guardians are expected to attend a 7 to 9:30 p.m., program starting off in the auditorium tomorrow evening. We plan to register each attendee as a PTO member; conduct a program in the auditorium; have group tours of the library, cafeteria, science lab, and new gym facilities; and return to the auditorium for a Q and A period. The faculty will be responsible for the actual tour of facilities; however, guides will be needed for the round-robin movement of the groups to these locations.

Your students did a fine job supporting this event last year; therefore, I would appreciate your providing the color guard as usual to post the flags, as well as some of the cadets to support this special program by helping out at the parking lot, manning the registration table, and serving as ushers and guides. I should mention that several of the older persons attending may need wheel chairs.

The assistant principal, Ms. Givens, will brief you on the schedule for the tours of campus facilities, and will be available to answer any questions you may have.

Thank you,
Ron Devers

The newly assigned colonel read this letter to the class that included the senior cadet leadership. Several of the upper class members who had participated in this event a year earlier asked that they be allowed to plan and conduct the exercise as they had done previously without instructor input. In approving their request, the Colonel stated that while he believed they would be able to repeat the previous year's satisfactory performance, and that he felt the support tasking would give him an opportunity to pass on some points he intended to make during the next week's training sessions on effective management..

At the class following the orientation program, the Colonel informed the class that he had received a glowing report from the principal, and gave his personal thanks to the unit for its outstanding support of the event. After personally congratulating the cadet leader for the positive steps he took in organizing and planning for this support tasking, he mentioned that several minor missteps were brought to his attention, and that he was of the opinion that some life skills could be developed by examining them.

Scenario B: (The Show And Tell Conference)

While informing the class that despite the impression their work had made on the principal, he mentioned that they should know also that several faculty members and several parents had rendered their congratulations on the cadets fine performances. Then, after stating that an after action report would normally be rendered after such an event was conducted, he mentioned again the need to examine the missteps observed that would normally be entered on such a report. He stated that because these observations subtracted somewhat from the total effort, they were worth examining in order to see if the class would benefit from discussing them as a group.

Using the overhead projector to display the notes he had made concerning the reports brought to his attention, he challenged the cadets to discuss them in the open. His stated goal was to see how close the class would come to matching his views on how the negative aspects of these could be avoided in the future. (See Figure 1.)

Figure 1: Observations

1: Information Breakdown. Two of the color guard members did not get the word on wearing white gloves; and one who had left his boots at home had to participate in unshined boots that were issued at the last minute. The color guard commander misunderstood the starting time, and arrived an hour and fifteen minutes too early.

2: Friction occurred between team members (2 incidents). One cadet reported being upset because the cadet commander chewed her out for leaving her post and stepping outdoors, and ordered her to return to duty at the reception desk immediately. Another, a cadet guide, reported that while she was not to blame, the cadet commander badgered her for not following the route designated for guiding a group of parents from the cafeteria to the science lab.

3: Lost car keys. One elderly grandmother became distressed after being unable to find her car keys that were dropped in the dark; and not knowing who to turn to, she screamed out for someone to help her. The parking lot crew could offer no help,; however, the keys were found by another attendee who returned from his car with a flashlight.

4: Wheel chair ramp door locked. The 10 minutes it took to locate the janitor to open the door leading from the wheelchair ramp to the main hallway was frustrating to an elderly attendee.

5: Short equipment and supplies. Some of the attendees did not get the Fact Sheet handout prepared by the school. Only 150 sheets had been printed in the initial batch, and the assistant principal did not bring additional copies to the registration desk until all visitors were in the auditorium. Also one of the registration lines was halted for a while until a parent donated a pen to replace the ballpoint pen that ran out of ink.

After presiding over animated student discussions pertaining to what could have been done during the planning and organization phases to eliminate the problems listed in *Figure 1* above, the instructor displayed a second chart containing his notes entitled *"Comments on Negative Observations."* The purpose of these comments was to allow the cadets to see how closely their earlier remarks had matched those shown, and to serve as lessons pertinent to organizing well. (See Figure 2.)

Figure 2: Comments On Negative Observations

1. Information Breakdown. Organizing requires that the most important considerations be stated in writing and provided to organizational leaders and sub-leaders. This should be done in order to insure that subordinate leaders are given key organizing and planning details, and to guard against information breakdowns. In this case, the document developed should have addressed the following: 1) the overall mission; 2) the uniform and dress requirements, to include detailed descriptions of the uniform for special teams; 3) the time for the initial assembly of participants; the start and end times of the program being supported; and the time and location from which all participants will be released from their duties.

2. Friction occurred between team members (2 incidents). In both these cases, in trying to insure that all participants were doing their jobs properly, the overall leader took it upon himself to correct what he believed to be the shortcomings of a team member not under his direct control. The lesson this incident provides is that since leaders of each task group were responsible for all their group did or failed to do, the better choices open to the commander were: 1) consult with the task leader, and 2) to ask questions before taking direct action. If he had done so in these cases, he would have found out that the cadet who had stepped outside was given permission to do so by her sub-leader because she had been feeling faint; and he would have learned that the cadet taking the different route was instructed to do so by the principal in order to avoid his group from passing through another that had paused in the hallway along the designated route.

3. Lost car keys. Both visibility and climate are important aspects for leaders to consider when determining a unit's special clothing and equipment needs. Because they had to work during darkness, luminous jackets and flashlights should have been issued to members of the parking lot support unit.

4. Wheel chair situation. When equipment is to be provided by an outside source, team leaders should be concerned with where the equipment is located, how it will be used, and how it will be returned to the supplier. In this case, a training session for the task group members concerned with using wheel chairs would have been in order. If there had been an opportunity to rehearse earlier, a walk-through prior to the start of the support event would have allowed the team to check out the equipment as well as the availability and suitability of the route designated to be used.

5. Short equipment and supplies. The organizing act requires that sufficient equipment and supplies needed to complete a tasking be on hand early, to include back-up items that are critical for task completion. As for these items, an inventory list should be made by teams to check their status prior to and at the end of a support tasking. At the end of the tasking, a report should be given the overall leader concerning the status of items issued. Further, when items are to be returned to providers, records should be maintained showing the time of return and the signature or initials of the persons who received the returned items.

<u>Scenario C</u>: (A View Of The Problem Fix)

At the next class meeting, after the students expounded on the learning value stemming from the review of the parent night support project, they were asked if they could think of anything that would have made the support tasking easier. The task leader, stating that he understood that it would have been better if he had made copies of the notes he had developed for his verbal briefing, asked if there was more if there was more i\he could have done in his regard?

The instructor responded by saying that this question was in line with the point he was intending to emphasize. This point was that putting things in writing when organizing for complex events was essential. He mentioned that the purpose of the documents developed would be to insure the requirements of the overall event were clear, and to assist participants in understanding their duties and responsibilities. He went on to say that organizing excellence is achieved when such notes establish authority and communication lines, designate those to be coordinated with, and list assignments and special instructions that will help others in carrying out acts having to do with the remaining four management principles that come into play, namely—planning, directing, coordinating, and controlling.

After stating that an organizing leader would do well to develop two documents—one that is strictly informational, and another that is task directed, he displayed an example of the first of these on the projection screen. He then made note of how the use of acronym SALUTE—given the students at an earlier time as a useful format for rendering an action report—was employed during the development of the General Statement he had made for the support overview. (See Item 1 in Figure 3.)

Figure 3: Support Overview—July 26 Parent Night Program

S (Size); **A** (Activity); **L** (location); **U** (Unit); **T**_(Time); **E** (Equipment)

I. <u>General</u>. **(S)** Over 200 parents and guardians are expected **(A)** to attend a Parent Orientation Program **(L)** in the school auditorium **(U)** sponsored by the PTA **(T)** from 7 to 9:30 p.m., on Tuesday, July 26, 20__. **(E)** Members of the Junior ROTC class will support the program utilizing equipment and materials provided by the JROTC department and the school.

II. <u>Mission</u>. The Junior ROTC department will support the parent night program by having cadets post the colors; man the registration desk; establish a parking lot detail; provide ushers for the auditorium; and provide guides for tours of school facilities.

III. <u>Responsibilities</u>. Overall responsibility for this tasking is given the cadet leader, who will be assisted by designated members of the headquarters element and by leaders of the 4 teams to be employed (see Unit Tasking Chart). All cadets, except color guard members who will be in ceremonial attire, will wear the summer uniform. Element leaders are responsible for rehearsing their teams, and for coordinating with school officials for special equipment, supplies, and materials.

IV. <u>Support</u>:

-- Ms. Givens will instruct the registration desk support team on their procedures, and provide programs, route maps for the special school tours, and money for making change.

-- The school nurse will provide 2 wheel chairs, and instruction on wheel chair operations.

-- The chief custodian will provide flashlights and luminous jackets for the parking lot detail.

After discussing the support overview document, the second document the instructor displayed on the projector screen was one he called a Unit Tasking Chart. Explaining that this format could be modified for use at any management level, he pointed out its value in arriving at a definition of the organizing act, and as an important assist for all those involved in the management acts that are integral to organizing for a project such as this; namely—planning, directing, coordinating, and controlling. After stating that this document was an example of a near-completed unit tasking chart, he explained the value of adding notes to it, and cautioned the cadets to remember that charts of this nature are always headed by a mission statement. (See *Figure 4*)

Figure 4: Unit Tasking Chart

Mission: The JROTC department will support the 7 to 9:30 p.m., Parent Night Program by posting colors; manning the registration desk; establishing a parking lot detail; providing ushers for the auditorium, and guides for tours of special school facilities.

Tm	Name	Job	Equipment Needed	Supplies Needed	Coordination Notes
A	John Mary Tom Bill	CG Leader Color Bearer Guard Guard	US Flag State Flag Rifle Rifle		Meet early at 6:30 p.m. Get white gloves from supply.
B	Susan Thomas Christa Crystal	Registration Leader Registrar Cashier Asst. Cashier	Radio Reg. Book	Pens (2) Notepads (2) Cash/and extra programs	Issue programs to all attendees. Collect and record fees from parents.
C	Don Mark Gil Unknown Unknown	Parking Lot Ldr Park Asst. Park Asst. Spec Tm Mbr Spec Tm Mbr	Radios (2) Clipboard Flash Lights (2) Wheel chairs (2) Luminous Jackets (2)	Notepad	See Custodian for flashlights & luminous jackets. See Nurse for wheel chairs.
D	Andy Keith Mona Sally Charles George Unknown (4)	Chief Usher Usher Usher Usher Chief Guide Guide Guides	Radios (2)	Extra Be Programs Route maps	available to direct people to seats, rest rooms, and to exits. Rehearse routes with guides.

> <u>Special Notes</u>: Team leaders are responsible for establishing procedures for completing team tasks; for the assembly, issue, and return of equipment and supplies; and for rehearsing their teams. Upon completion of this support task, all members will assemble in the JROTC office before being dismissed by the instructor.

Success-oriented individuals should note that a tasking chart begun early in the organizing stage will assist unit leaders in seeing the requirements clearly, and arranging to meet them. When used in initial briefings with team leaders, such a chart serves as an assist tool for determining if sufficient personnel and other resources are needed. A special feature of this particular chart is that it serves as a device to prompt sub-unit leaders to add the names of undesignated team members, and to designate responsibilities for: 1) picking up and signing for needed equipment and supplies, and 2) for the returning of supply and equipment items.

Summary

While each of the scenarios presented have their beginning in the first scenario with the message requesting support, the following information gathered from each scenario is significant:

From Scenario A, all should be able to gather that it is necessary to act upon the best method for doing a thing. In this case, the senior cadets, by insisting on conducting the program support using only their own experience base, could have made a better showing after seeking information from a management and leadership expert. Although the program support fully met the principal's expectations, the goal of all superior performers should be to exceed expected outcomes.

From Scenario B, it is clear that the missteps identified could have been avoided if the initial organizing session was established to address: 1) the leadership structure and it functions, 2) time and location issues, 3) clothing and equipment issues, 4) assembly points, 5) the methods of operation, and 6) questions concerning issues that had not been clarified.

From Scenario C, the value of developing two documents, 1) a written overview of the task to be completed in order to set the stage for assigning tasks, and 2) a tasking chart. It is felt that if handout sheets based on these document formats are utilized by organizers to disseminate information to unit leaders, they will set themselves apart as superior organizers.

Five Essentials for Organizing Excellence

1. <u>Put overall important things in writing</u>. These things should include the overall task or mission, a list of special tasks, the assembly time and place, and notes concerning dress requirements.
2. <u>Select task leaders for each special task</u>. In so doing, the overall leader narrows his span of control, removes the ambiguity from task requirements, and establishes a chain of communication.
3. <u>Provide resources for each team</u>. Since the resources available to any unit are time, people, money, equipment, facilities, and supplies, thought must be given to providing sufficient personnel and other resources to each team. It is essential that all resource items, including those to be acquired from others, are to be listed.
4. <u>Make a List questions still outstanding</u>. Even when mission assignment details have been thoroughly outlined, leaders can expect questions to arise in the categories of who, what, when, where, why, and how many. When answers cannot be provided early, these questions must be repeated and answers to them must be provided at a final coordination meeting.
5. <u>Issue special instructions to each team</u>. Although special instructions are directive in nature, they assist teams in understanding what is expected of them.

The 5 Essentials for Organizing Excellence should be made part of the portfolio of all who wish to better themselves in this arena. When armed with these essentials and with the tools for placing them into written formats, these individuals will find themselves ready to deal successfully with even complex organizing schemes.

CHAPTER X

ON THE ART AND SCIENCE OF TEACHING

For those concerned with the learning of others under their sphere of influence

If we are so far behind other countries in educating our students, why don't we reform our system by conducting studies to find out what the best of these other countries are doing, and implementing their methods? Don't we understand that by putting aside the current impetus on testing, and returning to the classical protocol for teaching well—that included a review of testing instruments, and re-teaching if necessary— our students' testing scores will improve and the problems plaguing our schools and universities will automatically disappear?

I have addressed the questions above in my briefings to educational leaders at various levels, in my success books, and in other attempts to enter the conversation on education reform. While many of my views are highlighted profusely on my website, www.allaroundsuccessbook.com, I maintain that poor teaching practices and neglected supervisory practices are at the heart of the problem. Unfortunately my research has led me to believe that even if solutions to the problems that beset us in being more effective were artfully presented, institutional policies would cause them to be summarily rejected. For some unexplained reason, these policies uphold the status quo, and guard against innovations designed to make improvements to the educational landscape.

That said, my views on the art and science of teaching well are based on the belief that those who wish to be seen as good teachers must see the art and science of it with the same insightfulness as do winning coaches who mentor cross country or golf teams. These coaches, before passing on strategies and tips to team members, first inquire into the minds of the designers who laid out the courses in order to have an explicit idea of how each should be tackled from start to finish. Likewise, it is of paramount importance for those in the teaching profession to study the designers' map, so to speak, and look to institute tried and true methods for helping others in plowing through their lessons.

This chapter is intended to provide food for thought for all who find themselves in the role of helping others to learn by emphasizing things that are not covered in training courses. With more families opting for "home learning," the discussions presented on the topics below are seen as important to their efforts as well:

- The Classroom Management Imperative
- The Presentation of Instruction
- The Lesson Outline with Notes
- Fail-safeness in Presenting a Class
- What Remarkable Teachers Understand and Do
- A Wholesome Learning Fix

The Classroom Management Imperative

While managing the classroom and presenting instruction are the two major responsibilities of the classroom teacher, it is not difficult to discern which responsibility trumps the other as a priority. This is so because the environment must be controlled consistently in order for effective teaching to take place. Effective teachers understand that it is imperative to control all that goes on in the classroom, and they work to do so by establishing standard classroom management procedures. Ideally, these include having: 1) a seating plan, 2) a non-wavering daily procedure for doing business, 3) classroom rules, and 4) a controlled discussion process.

The development of a seating plan for each class is essential for fast attendance taking and for various other controls. In addition, it is felt that a classroom-seating plan serves to encourage students to be in their seats at the appointed time, and to facilitate the assignment of group activities. Another important advantage is that such a plan serves to help visiting teachers interact with class members, and to make reports concerning the activities of the class members.

The establishment of a non-wavering procedure for conducting activities that recur on a daily or periodic basis is instituted within an essential management tool called the SOP. While a procedure for standardizing the manner in which recurring organizational issues are dealt with is useful for managers and leaders of all kinds, for teachers it serves as a control device, eliminates wasted time, and gives both teacher and students a model for dealing with issues involved in the business of learning.

Following is a classic example of a teacher putting certain SOP items in the context of rules:

"Students, as we are about to begin a journey on the road to your success, I must remind you that all journeys involving a group of people require an orderly system and rules of control if they are to be successful. As examples, 1) The old wagon trains heading West needed to have systems established for moving, for protection, for water consumption, etc. Most of you know that a wagon boss controlled these things. 2) A funeral procession moving from the church to the cemetery must have controls to keep it together so that all arrive at the same time. The convoy commander exercises control and direction in such an instance. Now, like both the wagon boss and convoy commander on our journey to success during this semester, my job is to keep us moving together in an orderly fashion. To do so, rules are necessary."

"My own rules are very simple: 1) be in your assigned seats when class begins, 2) raise hands in order to be recognized; 3) be respectful of others at all times; 4) give me your undivided attention when I ask for it; and 5) no clowning, as disruptive behavior will not be tolerated."

"For discussions—which we will do a lot of—the same rules apply. When our discussions are controlled by rules, positive things happen. As examples: (1) our behaviors can be put in check; (2) we can move from point to point without undue interruption; and (3) we can eliminate friction during the debates and discussions that will benefit each of us."

"If we commit to these rules, not only will we have grown together at the end of this journey, we will have developed knowledge and skills that will contribute to our success as a group, and each of you will become stronger in some way for the many journeys ahead."

The Presentation Of Instruction

> *Without a viable plan, a subject cannot be dealt with wholesomely*

The main problem with teaching is not so much that some teachers are not altogether familiar with the material they present, it is that they are not required to follow models established long ago for the presentation of instruction in such a way that both student progress and their own effectiveness can be determined by an evaluation using standard evaluation criteria.

While managing the classroom is essential to effective teaching, teachers who intend to set themselves apart as worthy guides understand that deliberate steps must also be taken in order to insure that every class they present will receive high marks were it to be evaluated. The most important of the steps taken by these teachers to failure-proof their presentations involves:

- Reviewing the student text, familiarizing themselves with the supporting resource book(s), and by following a regimen involving standard practices that have been established for the delivery, review, and evaluation of the information to be presented.

- Developing lesson objectives for each session, and personal guide notes to insure that key points are covered and that the class moves along in a semi-regimented fashion.

The semi-regimented fashion of delivery for each day's instruction is recommended due to the notion that every class presented should be a model of excellence. That is to say that if class presentations are to meet the criteria established for class evaluations, they should always have a standardized beginning, middle, and ending.

By a standard beginning, is meant to say that each class should be introduced formally. The recommended four-step introduction process involves:

1. Delivering an attention statement or ice-breaker.
2. Identifying the topic to be discussed.
3. Giving the purpose of the instruction.
4. Presenting the learning or lesson objectives.

By a structured middle, is meant to say that the two-step process should be used:

1. A proper lead-in to the body of the lesson.
2. The thorough development of each objective should be made before moving on.

By a standard ending, is meant to say that a conclusion phase should be reached consisting of a summary, a review of the objectives, a check-up, and a closing statement.

While presenting instruction in this manner is essential for teaching effectiveness, its major goals are to insure that real learning takes place, and that skills pertinent to increasing student achievement are imparted. Understanding this, the most effective teachers utilize a process for testing their students' grasp of material presented. They also take pains to review all tests and quizzes, re-teach when necessary, and look for opportunities to arm their students with critical thinking tools that are designed to facilitate their success during future evaluations.

The Lesson Outline With Notes

It is important for students to understand that lessons are presented in accordance with an outline, and that teachers usually follow the outline as planned. Their lesson outlines, when developed properly, always consist of 3 parts:

1. The introduction
2. The body
3. The conclusion

The introduction consists of 4 parts:

1. *The Attention Statement*: This can be a personal experience, an anecdote, a joke, a startling statement, a rhetorical question, a challenge, etc.
2. *The Topic:* This is the specific heading of the subject to be covered.
3. *The Purpose*: Even if not stated in a school-learning environment, the purpose of most lessons will be *to inform* the students.
4. *The Learning Objectives*: These are the specific things the students are expected to *be able to do* upon leaving the classroom.

The body consists of 2 parts:

1. *The lead-in*: It can be as simple as "We have identified 4 things we expect you to be able to do at the end of this class, so let's begin with breaking down the first of these."
2. *The development of the objectives*: When done properly, each objective identified will be developed in-turn with the idea that students will be able to deal with the objective as stated.

The conclusion consists of at least 4 parts:

1. *The Summary*. A presentation of the substance of the lesson delivered in a condensed form.
2. *A Review of the learning objectives*. A restatement of student expectations (what they were expected to be able to do at the end of the period of instruction.
3. *A Check-up*. A questioning process to determine how successful both students and teacher were in meeting their stated expectations.
4. *A Closing statement*. A comment that may include the teacher's observations, and that discloses the value of this lesson for future activities.

NOTES:

a. The learning objectives are the most important items entered on a lesson outline, as they serve to note what is to be evaluated later. They also serve to assist the teachers in checking to determine whether or not their own objectives were met. If not met, the teacher should plan to re-teach the parts that were not learned and/or to give homework that will pertain to the class objective(s) needing more emphasis.

b. It is important for the student to understand that all teachers do not use the format above as a guide for uniformly dealing with topics. In such cases, it is up to wise students to select what they believe they should be able to do as a result of a class of instruction, to determine what portions of the instruction will be evaluated at a later time, and to develop stratagems for being able to display their knowledge of the topic. These stratagems should be focused on the questions:

1) Why was this topic covered?
2) What ideas of value were presented by the author and teacher?
3) In what ways were these ideas meaningful or challenging?,
4) How can I reconstruct these ideas in terms that are simple to explain them in my own words?

Fail-Safeness In Presenting A Class

Presentations oriented to making high marks upon evaluation should be the objective

In an age where teacher effectiveness is often graded and made a part of their formal evaluations, teachers who wish to be seen as always effective should have a standard method for insuring the points they will be graded on are automatically covered with fail-safe stratagems for insuring that each class is controlled and presented skillfully. Assuming that the classroom management imperatives are in place, class evaluators cannot help but be impressed by presentations that are introduced properly and that include active student involvement throughout the presentation. I trained my teachers to be failsafe presenters by emphasizing that the first opportunity for scoring high on their evaluations and for displaying that they are skillful performers, is during the phase when the lesson is formally introduced.

<u>In Presenting The Introduction</u> Evaluators are impressed during the formal introduction when teachers demonstrate that they understand the parts of the introduction, make a point of involving students early in the lesson, and that they are skillful in asking questions. Good Teachers understand that while the most important part of the introduction pertains to the class learning objectives, this is the point where their skill in engaging students and employing the optimum questioning technique can be displayed. This process involves having two or more students read the learning objectives, followed by asking questions and pausing in such a way that each member of the class is moved to ponder them with the expectation of being called just before directing the question to a specific student (the ASK, PAUSE, CALL Method).

While effective teachers take pains to insure that the objectives are kept to a minimum, that they are realistic goals that are worthwhile and attainable, and that they are clearly understood, they leave the door open for displaying their questioning skills. Examples of questions to be asked concerning the objectives that will undoubtedly impress an evaluator are as follows: 1) "What is meant by the term "learning objectives?" 2) "Why is it important for the student to pay particular attention to the learning objectives of each class?"

<u>In Dealing With The Body of the Lesson</u>

Since the body of the lesson consists of two parts: 1) the lead-in, and 2) the part where each objective is developed, teachers display their skills by showing that they have artfully prepared their teaching points and by engaging students by way of asking of asking well-thought-out questions using the *Ask, Pause, Call* method.

<u>In Closing Out The Instruction Period</u>

Although it is not usually done, forward-thinking teachers may wish to dictate one or two thought-provoking questions for their students to write out and ponder on later before closing out the period of instruction. In ending the teaching session, the parts identified for the conclusions phase—the summary, the review of the objectives, and check-up to detect the existence of and confusing elements, must be covered just before a closing statement is made that puts a value on the session, and that may disclose teacher satisfaction with the instructional period.

What Remarkable Teachers Understand And Do

Dealing with the problems that plague learning communities is the first requirement

What Remarkable Teachers Understand

Remarkable teachers understand that their preparations have qualified them to teach, but that they must add to their studies in order to be expert practitioners. They also understand that although their preparatory raining was not so oriented, they must be poised to play a roles in allaying the main problems said to plague the school districts and some of the colleges. These problems have been identified as:

- Low attendance

- Dropouts and low graduation rates

- Low test scores

- Low GPA's

- Peer pressure and negative student-based behavior issues.

While educators generally agree that these five are the problems of deepest concern, they also agree that the solutions to the problems identified lies within the students themselves, and that if given the tips and strategies mentioned in wholesome fashion, the plaguing problems identified would be either reduced or alleviated. While the dropout rate and low test scoring are the two most mentioned in general conversations, remarkable teachers do not fail to see that since low test scoring is at the heart of the other four plaguing problems. Therefore, in an effort steps to empower their students with the critical thinking skills for being successful in their educational pursuits, they need to take deliberate steps to impart tips to make them high achievers.

In that the problems mentioned fall mainly in the students' domain, it can be readily assumed that most occur because the students involved have not been successful. It can be further assumed that they have not been successful because they have not been motivated mentally and morally; nor have they been given strategies that cause them to be more academically astute.

What Remarkable Teachers Do

Remarkable teachers do several things extremely well. Among these:
- they are consistent in merging classroom management and management of instruction imperatives so that they support and enhance the learning environment;
- they teach to learning objectives and work to see that these have been met satisfactorily by the end of the instructional period;
- they review learning assessment instruments and re-teach complex and hard to grasp issues revealed; and
- they are adept providing guidelines, formats, strategies, and tips for mastery of subject material.
- When possible, they pass on tips and strategies that give their students an edge in thinking critically, making informed decisions, setting, attainable goals, and operating successfully in the work environment.

A Wholesome Learning Fix

From my book of memoirs, "An Incredible Journey"

"In looking back over my life and contemplating the target in the success arena that ought to be engaged first and fixed, I would more than likely choose the art of teaching and the manner in which learning is impeded. In recent years I have become very vocal in pointing out that there is a great need to reform the educational landscape and deal realistically with the problems that plague our schools and universities. While these problems stem from the students not being successful, they would be more successful if: 1) given lessons that are prepared, presented, and evaluated in a fashion that make them more skilled performers; and 2) given tips pertaining to these lessons that impact positively on their outlooks towards success.

"Although impacting student outlooks may fall outside the province of teacher expectations, causing them to be more successful in class is something that teachers can do by changing their methods of delivering and evaluating instruction. In that they have not done so, I must conclude that the problem will not be fixed until teachers and their supervisors become aware of how things are best learned. In my view, what is missing is that that they do not provide the motivation for students to change their outlooks, nor do they commit to making student mastery of subject material as simple an uncluttered as possible.

"As I see this as being the seat of the trouble, as a first order of business I would propose that the methods now in vogue for of presenting and evaluating instruction be abandoned because they are not working. At present, the protocol is to teach, test, and assign grades; however, the problem arises when the lessons that are presented do not follow a structured order, are not based on student learning objectives, and when testing instruments are not purposely reviewed. Who can see the sense in a system based on the idea that students are being educated when methods for determining whether or not teaching objectives and student learning objectives have been reached are left out?

"The position I have been forced to hold is that when teachers commit to managing their classrooms with skill and to making student mastery of subject material as simple a process as possible, the problems mentioned will be alleviated, and both teachers and students will be more successful. Further, I believe the best way to promote learning is to begin with an explanation of the whole puzzle prior to breaking off the pieces and describing how they fit. In other words, I believe the most significant problems in helping others to learn will be alleviate when the holistic view—emphasizing a thorough description of the whole of a segment—is presented prior to presentations pertaining to the dependent or independent parts of the segment to be learned. And while this holds for learning in the general sense as I see it, my premise is debatable. Others may argue that learning is best promoted by challenging students and urging them to struggle and work hard on their own.."

"Nevertheless, if asked for my view on how things are best learned, I would offer the following as a wholesome learning fix:

'*Things are best learned when a picture of the major segment of the subject to be learned is shown first and explained in full. Then, before being put in their rightful places, the pieces of the thing are shown and explained with the same fullness as the whole. In this way the learner will be enabled to understand how the pieces fit, and can develop for himself stratagems for dealing with the functional aspects of the thing in a wholesome manner.'"*

"In addition to this, I would provide some examples that would help shed light on the position I have taken. These would include the following:

-- *'If parents were to give a child a total picture of how they see it acting and reacting as perfectly as possible, it will be easier to help the child with the pieces, such as, hygiene, obedience, personal safety, study, skill development, and his attitude and manners.'*
-- *'Although it has been alluded to earlier, the development of students' comprehension, reading, writing, and speaking skills would be enhanced if the basic model for each of these acts—the paragraph—was first discussed in detail.'*
-- *'In almost all learning processes a book or parts of it is utilized to support the lessons; however, nowhere in the curriculum is the idea of how a book is developed and how it is to be used, covered in detail. It stands to reason that if the whole of the book is covered within a lesson, followed by an examination of its parts, this will enable readers to establish a relationship with the author, and be better able to deal with the contents of the book.'*
-- *'It is a certainty that if the ideal classroom presentation was the first and primary focus in developing teachers, and if breaking down the parts of the teaching act with a focus on what is the most ideal method of demonstrating mastery of each part, more excellent teachers would be the result.'*
-- *'If a professor assisting a doctorial graduate student takes an example of the best dissertation available and explains its workings in full, and if he then breaks down the parts of it and gives the reason why these parts are ideal, would not the student be less apt to turn in a shoddy draft dissertation?'"*

"Although I could go on and on in this vein in speaking of almost any field of study, all this is to say that skill development is based on the acquisition of the sort of knowledge that pertains to the wholeness of something that may even be complex. This view supports the idea that while it is important for teachers to commit themselves to understanding the whole of a topic before engineering lessons that deal with the parts thereof, it just as important for individuals who wish to become better in developing themselves to commit to bringing the holistic view into play for further study as soon as possible."

> While making measured steps and strides in getting to the house one is most interested in are important, knowing about the pillars the house rests upon, its rooms, and what they contain is of greatest value.

CHAPTER XI

ON SUCCEEDING IN THE WORKING ENVIRONMENT

Who has the best chance of succeeding in the working environment?

The question above is a tricky one to answer because it depends on how one defines success in the working environment. While some may think the that those individuals imbued with the spirit to work hard and skillfully at a job they understand will have the best chance, others will think that this is not necessarily so. Although both sides will agree that those so imbued will normally be seen as valuable employees, those believing that more is needed think that the ones in this group who are also aware of the fundamental elements for getting a job, and the timehonored practices for successfully dealing with people and workforce issues, are more likely to not only keep their jobs, but also to be considered for higher positions within a field of work.

While the topics entitled *"The Groups Of People in Our Lives"* and *"People Within The 3 Levels Of Activity In All Organizations"* in the chapter "On Being Better" speaks expressly to the knowledge and life skill issues involved, I believe that individuals concerned about what it takes to be real successful in the working environment will benefit from the offering in this chapter. This belief is based first on my thinking that the impression individuals make when applying for and interviewing for a position is a lasting impression, and that this impression sets the stage for future judgments concerning their potential within an organization. The second basis for this belief pertains to the thought that when individuals are armed with knowledge about getting and keeping a job are more able to assimilate sets of fundamental workforce practices that serve to mark them as candidates for upward movement.

In understanding the volatility of the market, I believe that this chapter is important for those who may be seeking new employment opportunities, or even new ways to show themselves as valuable employees. While the meaningfulness of first impressions cannot be overstated, individuals with the goal of moving upwards in an organization should be aware of how build upon this impression. These should know that first sign of their potential value is provided in a professionally rendered resume; that the next sign is provided by the applicant's performance during the interview process; and that the third important sign has to do with saying and doing the things that mark one as special.

While the first three items below are skewed toward the aspect of obtaining a job position, the last article listed below is intended to round out the discussion on what individuals need to understand and do in order to reach their success goals in the 21st Century's job market.

These are:

- <u>The Resume and Cover Letter</u>
- <u>The Top 12 Interviewing Tips</u>
- <u>Special Tips on Job Interviewing</u>
- <u>Helpful Hints For On The Job</u>.

The Resume And Cover Letter

The Resume

Below are listed the standard parts of the resume. It should be noted that samples of resumes showing how these parts may be entered on the resume are easily found on the Internet and in reference libraries.

<u>Your Address Block</u> Name
    Address
    Phone or cell number and E-mail address

<u>Education:</u>
    List schools attended and any awards or honors.

<u>Experience:</u>
    List work history. If none, it's OK to list volunteer work like car washing, cutting lawns, or even baby-sitting.
    List companies worked for separately with dates of employment for each, including the positions you held or job titles.
    List your responsibilities in bullet form.

<u>References:</u>
    If references are not listed, it is OK to merely state: REFERENCES ON REQUEST. In such a case, however, the applicant should have a list with names and telephone numbers of references on hand to give interviewers upon request.

The Cover Letter

Below are listed the standard parts of the cover letter to resumes. It should be noted that samples of cover letters showing how these parts may be entered on the letter are easily found on the Internet and in reference libraries.

<u>Your Address Block</u> (Use same address block as on the resume)

<u>Date</u> (Use actual date of mailing)

<u>Company Address Block</u> (With name and title of the company contact person)

<u>Body Of Letter</u> (Let the employer know what position you are applying for, how you learned of it, and why the employer should select you for an interview).

<u>Complimentary Close</u> (Example: *Respectfully yours,*)

<u>Signature Block</u> (Your hand written signature written neatly over your typed signature)

The Top 12 Interviewing Tips

Be ready to make a good impression

1. Take A Copy Of Your Resume With You.
2. Be Cognizant Of Key Information About The Company.
3. Gather Copies Of Transcripts And References To Bring Along.
4. Get A Good Night's Sleep.
5. Eat A Small Snack To Control Stomach Rumbling.
6. Be Dressed, Groomed And Ready For The Interview.
   - If formal, wear appropriate attire. If informal, wear a conservative long-sleeved shirt or blouse (white is best, pastel is next best).
   - Insure shoes are conservative, clean, and polished.
   - Have a well-groomed hairstyle.
   - Insure fingernails are clean and trimmed.
   - Have no visible body piercings (nose ring, eyebrow rings).
   - Insure cologne or perfume are minimized.
   - Empty pockets of large objects or loose coins.
   - Avoid habits that may be distracting (gum chewing, smoking).
   - Take a light briefcase or portfolio case (optional).

7. Arrive 5-10 Minutes Early At The Interview Site.
8. Bring Pens And Paper.
9. Go Alone (No Children, Friends, Etc.)
10. Use A Firm Handshake, And Maintain A Pleasant Appearance .
11. When You Do Not Understand A Question, Do Not Fail To Say So.
12. Answer All Questions As Directly A Possible; However, Do Not Offer More Information Than Is Necessary.

Special Tips On Job Interviewing

Sell yourself
---

1. Brush up on some language concepts you know will be needed during the interview, to include those for meeting people, answering questions, being unable to answer questions, being grateful, and for ending a meeting.
2. Plan to arrive AT LEAST 5-10 minutes early for your interview.
3. Start and end your interview with a good firm handshake; be energetic, full of life. Never be *just an applicant* or *just another job seeker.*
4. Be as courteous and polished as you know how in your mannerisms.
5. Always look at the person to whom you are talking; follow his eyes.
6. Be a relaxed, cool and calm person of interest.
7. Don't try to push yourself too fast; and be more on the humble, rather than on the aggressive side.
8. Know as much about the firm as possible. If you know only a little about the firm, be honest enough to say so, *if asked.*
9. Do not brag, but be prepared to explain your qualifications, and why you think you would be a valuable employee.
10. Sell yourself. Try to get every employer to offer you the job you are seeking, or to offer you another within the firm.
11. Exhibit a willingness to prove your worth to the company by making it clear that you will work diligently.
12. Be natural; do not present a pre-rehearsed appearance.
13. Keep an open mind and listen with great interest; but *never jot down notes during your interview.*
14. Be prepared to ask several questions, e.g., the size of the company, its major locations, and the promotional opportunities associated with the position you are applying for.
15. At the end, be sure to thank the persons conducting the interview for the opportunity of interviewing for the job.

Helpful Hints For On The Job

Strategies for moving onward and upward

---

1. Be diligent and thorough in adhering to your supervisor's actions, orders, and policies.
2. If in doubt about understanding parts of a task assignment, seek advice from the task giver.
3. When receiving a complicated task to accomplish, make sure there is no misunderstanding before leaving the task-giver.
4. When given a number of additional tasks to complete, seek approval to follow your updated priority list for completing projects.
5. Inform your boss when tasks are completed. Do the same when task completion is impeded for any reason.
6. In an office situation where your comments and reports have been misconstrued, be diligent in seeking to determine how they became so. Apologize for any confusion you may have caused.
7. When time is of essence and changes must be made, receive approval for proceeding along the lines you believe will suffice for completing assigned projects.
8. When time is of essence for developing an important document, do not delay by attempting to finalize it; take drafts dealing with key issues to your supervisor for review as early as possible.
9. When a task becomes too difficult, seek help from your immediate supervisor if available. If not, seek help from your approving authority.
10. It is not advisable to trust your own reading of a document you developed that may reflect on your organization; therefore, insist upon having a good writer review a hard copy of your composition.
11. Do not transmit messages to others in lateral or higher positions and to other organizations without your supervisor's approval.
12. Never engage in oral arguments of any kind, speak unkindly of another, or show anger.
13. All persons and all organizations will be evaluated; therefore, determine the criteria for your personal evaluation, as well as for your portion of the team's or the organization's evaluation.
14. In all your dealings be fair, truthful, and as cheerful as possible.
15. Use terms like:
    - "I have no problem with that (except)…"
    - "I can live with that." "I'm open to another opinion."
    - "Is that subject still open?"
    - "I had hoped that subject was closed."
    - "I hope you feel better."
    - "We will get it done."
    - "May I ask a question?"
    - "I need help in understanding …"

CHAPTER XII

PUTTING IT ALL TOGETHER

With positive thinking and confidence building devices

"Of the many things that I have learned during my many years on this planet, one that is the most profound is that it is a difficult thing to improve others with one's word or actions. As I have found this to be especially so in the success arena, what emerges is the notion that although mentors – even tall tree mentors – may be on hand for empowering others, they are seldom turned to for this purpose; they impart skills mainly by their examples and by passing on tips and strategies. Believing this is the case, I believe also that few will sit still to be nurtured by another, and that those who become better practitioners as a result of their fleeting relationships with wise others, do so by a process I would call 'self-mentoring.'"

The caption above is taken from my book of memoirs during my discussion on the educational communities' pitfalls and how to correct them by way of reforming the system. In the last paragraph of this discussion I went on to say:

> *"The conclusion I have drawn from a lifetime of watchfulness is that education is only one of the fields that must be plowed with straighter rows. Our thinking and our actions in these arenas must evolve in such a way that our programs are strictly success-oriented and presented by well prepared teachers who may be equated to fruit-bearing trees. If the important fields are cultivated in this way, it is certain that those who hunger to better themselves in any arena can pluck from these the fruit they, themselves, can process via the self-mentoring technique in order to grow taller and more powerful."*

After reading this it should come as no surprise that my thinking is that "being a better you" can only be accomplished by the individual who is not only committed to the notion of becoming better, but also who realizes that becoming better in any arena is done only by way of a selfmentoring process. While I believe there is some value in receiving tips and strategies for dealing with concepts and skills such as those pertaining to writing, problem-solving, decisionmaking, organizing, or any game or vocation – until the tips and strategies offered are internalized and adapted for a person's use, they have little to do with one's "being a better you."

In planning this chapter, my objective was to serve up again a number of those things highlighted earlier that will assist those inclined to better themselves to feel that they have been becoming better since reading the first page of this book. But more than this, since more is required, I am unable to say with certainty that "you are now armed sufficiently for 'being a better you.'" Instead, the following *30 Failsafe Tips In A Nutshell* are presented as offerings to be processed utilizing the self-mentoring technique. While these have been amalgamated with much of what has gone before, I am confident that upon adapting these for your personal use the positive thinking and confidence building you will have achieved will astound you and those around you.

30 Failsafe Tips In A Nutshell

Tools for winning friends and influencing others

These 30 tips were developed in an effort to combine elements pertinent to each topic so that the topic could be expressed in a few words. While neither tip is intended to be as complete or profound as possible, each has been placed in capsule form for the purpose of clarifying their nature and use in dealing with a wide variety of personal and interpersonal challenges. While each is written to serve as irrefutable talking points, they are intended to serve also as prompts and guidelines for a wide range of acts that have not been addressed in this way before in a single volume.

ON BEHAVING: In that behavior is defined as the actions or reactions of persons or things to external or internal stimuli, it can be expected that those who are mindful of the definition are more likely to take care concerning what they say and do than those who are not. It follows that those so aware have come to understand that their behavior will always be in check if they are considerate of others, considerate of their manners, and if they commit to adhering to the other personal guidelines illustrated in the pieces in this book entitled, *"Lifetime Keys for Personal Success," "The My and Our Rule," "The Kindergarten Experience,"* and *"The Boy and Girl Scout Laws."* While these guidelines apply mainly in the personal arena, forward thinkers will have a decided edge in the reputation-building arena when they adopt both these, and arm themselves with the tenets of behavior that may be gleaned from the pieces devoted expressly to building up interpersonal skills. These are entitled, *"The Groups of People in Our Lives and Our Concerns," "People Within the 3 levels Of Activity In All Organizations,"* and *"The Four Color Personality Groups Of people In Our Lives."*

ON COMPREHENDING: In order for something to be done well, the first requirement is that it be understood. When dealing with a process, idea, or problem that is difficult to understand, a recommended method is to see the whole of it as a puzzle with sections consisting of identifiable pieces or parts that can be broken down and studied. When steps are taken to connect the pieces of each section together and link the sections together in an orderly fashion, the nature and function of all the parts involved are more easily grasped and explained.

ON CONTROLLING: Organizational controls are put in place mainly for orderliness, security, and safety, by those who are concerned about resource conservation. These are usually backed up by a system in which procedures, regulations, standards, and monitoring devices play huge roles. In controlling people resources, 3 styles of leadership are employed by wise leaders. *The directing style* is implemented for task accomplishments when time is of essence, and when subordinates require direct supervision and control. *The delegating style* is utilized when subordinate leaders are well trained, and are capable of seeing that tasks are accomplished without supervision by the primary leader. *The participating style* is used in cases when the primary leader believes that doing so is necessary for task accomplishment, or when his involvement is centered on testing and improving organizational procedures. While wise leaders implement systems designed to prevent loss of control, they take pains to never over-control.

ON COORDINATING: Coordination measures are put in place to establish harmonious relationships and to avoid conflict and confusion when two are more organizations must work closely together during operations that may be complicated. Wise coordinators take pains to review potential problem areas with their counterparts, and take steps to insure that these are provided details that include names, locations, contact points, and emergency contact measures.

ON DECIDING: Whether rendered as personal judgment or as a recommendation for an activity in the managerial arena, all decisions should be based on a thought process designed to arrive at the action that will deliver the desired results. Decision makers think first of what they wish to accomplish, while considering the problems that may impact on their efforts. Then, because there will always be more than one way to do a thing, they take steps to choose the option that is best for reaching the objective and conserving organizational and other resources. Wise decision makers always consider worst-case scenarios, and have well thought out contingency or back-up plans.

ON DREAMING: Making dreams come true begins with setting goals that are realistic, attainable, worthwhile, measurable, and time-bound. The process continues with plans to make both short term and long-term goals come true. Wise dreamers put sub-goals in writing and take steps to monitor their progress and to see if they are still on track in their quests towards goal achievements.

ON INTERVIEWING: Making a good impression during the interviewing process depends not only on how one acts and speaks, serious job seekers also dress appropriately, display good manners, and take steps to show their fitness for employment and their potential value to the organization. Serious job seekers will have an edge on others in presenting these qualities if they review both *"The Top 12 Interviewing Tips"* and *"Facts On Job Interviewing,"* and if they adopt the strategies implied in both documents as integral to their interviewing regimen.

ON LEADING: Leading well requires the acts of influencing others to meet objectives in a timely fashion, while keeping them oriented and well informed. Effective leaders understand that in improving their organizations their main responsibilities involve the training, discipline, and employment of their subordinates. They make decisions based on problem-solving and decision-making strategies, and they commit themselves to the following: standardizing procedures for recurring activities, applying the principles of leadership diligently, demonstrating the traits that signal good character, using the indicators of leadership to determine the status of their own effectiveness, training their units as a team to meet individual and unit evaluation criteria, and looking for opportunities to practice and rehearse plans and emergency situations. Wise leaders also look for the good in dissenting opinions, and utilize the worst-case scenario method while developing plans to handle difficult situations and emergencies.

ON LEARNING: While the act of gaining knowledge involves being studious, open minded, and curious, effective learners take pains to develop good study habits and techniques, take and keep good notes; maintain a personal notebook (GEM Book) containing items that may be useful in future ventures;

and utilize the dictionary, reference library, and the Internet in advancing their knowledge base. Likewise, individuals concerned with advancing their skill base, area careful to review the fundamentals that apply to the whole of their craft, adopt sound measures for dealing with the parts of greatest concern, and establish sound practice regimens.

ON LIVING: Those who wish to live rewarding lives do not take themselves too seriously, but strive to be happy. They avoid tendencies toward selfishness at all costs, and are goal-oriented. Living is made easier when people understand the need to tolerate and deal with others wisely; seek advice concerning things in which they have little or no skill; and copy admirable attributes of strong others. As a part of having a purposeful life, individuals take action to insure that matters pertaining to the health, safety, security, and well being of those they are responsible for are covered. While the idea of living well may involve having the home, family, friends, and the finances one may hope for, it is important to remember that these are of little comfort unless they are accompanied by the piece of mind that comes with having been true to oneself, and having played the many games of life with the skillfully and fairly.

ON LOVING: In that the act of loving has to do with the actions or reactions of persons to external or internal stimuli, it follows that attempts to define love will lead to it being placed squarely in the behavior domain. When love is seen as a behavior, it follows that it involves the manner in which individuals behave properly in dealing with themselves, with others, and with things within their sphere of concern. With this view of the loving act, individuals can teach others what love means and how to evaluate it. Another important aspect of this view is that it allows individuals to determine if aspects of their behavior towards certain others and objects fall in the category of non-loving expressions that are in need of correction.

ON MANAGING: The art of management involves the skillful application of 5 principles, namely— planning, organizing, directing, coordinating, and controlling. While all managers are concerned with the utilization and control their own resources, including: time, money, equipment, materials, facilities, and the people they are responsible for, big business managers are concerned mainly with the effect of these as they pertain to the conservation of, or the growth of the organization's finances. Good managers define themselves by making well thought out decisions concerning resource utilization by establishing standard procedures for recurring activities involving them. These also take steps to train their subordinates to meet and exceed organizational expectations, look for opportunities to rehearse key evaluation measures, and work to insure that all involved are able to satisfactorily meet the criteria that will be tested upon formal organizational evaluations.

ON MODELING: Assuming that a model is always useful in testing or perfecting a final product, it follows that individuals with a quest for improving themselves will not shy away from seeking models for doing so. This is why wise individuals do not hesitate in copying and improving upon the admirable attributes they see in others that can be made to fit within their own personalities and abilities. Wise individuals are also industrious in looking for and developing models and formats for doing things of importance as skillfully as possible.

ON OBEYING: Being obedient is more than being instant in responding after being told the first time to correct something. While one aspect of it has to do with following an accepted protocol on a consistent basis, another has to do with being instant in doing things correctly without being told. An example of something that should never be done is when an individual within an organization commits to doing a certain thing because it make sense to him or her while being aware that the act is in deference to approved rules and procedures. Such an individual will be not be seen as industrious, but as an incompetent rule breaker. Instead of implementing a procedure believed to be superior to one in place, wise individuals understand that the perceived procedure should first be presented to the approving authority in the form of a sound recommendation. In a case where a rule is inadvertently broken, wise individuals issue an apology for doing so, and commit to not breaking that rule again.

ON ORGANIZING: Being able to organize with skill is foundational to good managers and leaders. These understand that the basic requirements for organizing include the development of a mission statement for what is to be done, the appointment of leaders, the assignment of tasks, and the dissemination of resources to those who are to do the work. Wise organizers also understand that the essential things should be put in writing, that all resource items utilized in support of operations should be accounted for and returned to their places, and that a final report concerning task accomplishment to include problems encountered and recommendations for future activities should be submitted to the task developer.

ON PARENTING: In that the home is microcosmic of the world outside, parents must see themselves as the bows that send the arrows—their own children—out from the home with the best skills they can provide for surviving in a complex world. Good parenting requires that children are given a place of their own within the family construct, quality time with parent figures, the assignment of chores that are skill producing and meaningful, a vested interest in the child's wholesome development for the future. This includes: training that pertains to proper mannerisms in dealings with others; the administering of rewards for proper conduct, and the delving out of punitive measures for breaches of established conduct rules; the scheduling of worthwhile activities; and the establishment of realistic and attainable goals.

ON PEOPLE: Wise individuals understand that people are different from themselves, and that they owe certain things to the three groups of people that will always be in their personal and business lives. They understand that people within these groupings have definite personality colors, and that the distinctive features of the four major personality colors must be allowed for in dealing with them personally and within organizations. Wise individuals also understand that people who are the most revered are those who are oriented to making a real difference in the lives of others.

ON PLANNING: Planning is a management principle that is foundational to both managers and leaders. These understand that a mission statement and an estimate of the situation are crucial to the implementation of formal planning activities. They understand that these activities always include: tasks for the major organizations involved; instructions to eliminate confusion and to assist units involved in coordinating their efforts; roles to be played by the elements providing supplies and other logistical support; and information concerning communications networks that will be utilized, and special methods in place to contact leaders. Wise planners work to insure that subordinate leaders are given initial planning guidelines as early as possible. These distinguish themselves by considering worst-case scenarios and by developing contingency plans to handle potential problematic situations.

ON READING: The ability to read well is based on skills that will allow the individual to comprehend the ideas being presented in the material being read. As ideas are presented in paragraphs, good readers always look for the sentence expressing the main idea and observe how the idea is supported with details that provide facts, explanations, examples, etc. When reading to absorb material that will be tested, wise readers decide on whether their purpose is to acquire facts, ideas, or explanations. They look up the meanings of all new words, make notes concerning how ideas are connected, and underline important passages needing to be reread for clarity's sake. They also think about the order in which passages were developed and how they fit into the writer's stream of thought before going on to new materials.

ON REMEMBERING: Being able to call to mind important occurrences, dates, locations, lessons, ideas, etc., is sometimes difficult for the old and young. Because memory oversights can sometimes be costly, wise individuals understand the importance of using notes to prompt remembering things that may be lost due to time lags and other reasons. These utilize other memory aids to include: establishing files for permanent records; maintaining a 'things to do" list for tasks they intend to accomplish; and utilizing calendars to mark upcoming events and the requirements concerning said events.

ON REPORTING: As it is a mark of high achievers, the importance of giving accurate and timely reports cannot be over emphasized. Individuals should internalize personal formats for standard and incident reports, and take care to report when a task has been completed. When reporting the incidence of a negative situation to a superior, it is a good idea to have a recommendation in mind for fixing the problem.

ON SPEAKING: While it may be true that one's actions speak louder than one's words, what one says is a behavior that is a sign of one's character; therefore, one should take care to speak in a formal setting only when he or she really has something to say. Wise speakers think first, and determine if the initial thought that comes to mind is what they mean, if it should be discarded or rephrased, or if there is a more appropriate way to communicate it. They also understand that impulse or reactive-speech in heated situations do not bear good results, and that prompt notes are useful when speaking to formal groups.

ON SPENDING: The power of thought should always be used before spending your time, energy, or money. Wise individuals keep records of the status of their finances, do not spend more than they earn, do without things that are unnecessary, and avoid spending systems that are designed to make others wealthy at their expense.

ON STUDYING: Studying is a recurring event; therefore, a standardized procedure should be established for doing it. The wise understand that careful study is a work in progress where the purpose in doing so is the first consideration. Study should be done at times and in places where distractions are minimized, and when one's full attention can be devoted to applying the techniques that will render the clearest picture of what is to be understood.

ON SUCCEEDING: In that success is the achievement of something desired, planned, or attempted, it is clear that one cannot consider that he or she has succeeded in something unless a dream or goal has been reached. Therefore, wise persons work to implement the goal-setting process, develop strategies and plans for reaching the objective sought, and work out methods to be used in making each aspect of their success plans a reality.

ON TEACHING: While it is clear that formal teaching is a three-part process involving the passing on of information using an introduction, body, and conclusion, the most important aspect deals with what the students should be able to do at the end of the class. As this aspect will be the basis on which evaluation materials are developed, teachers will do well to determine their own effectiveness by examining the extent the stated learning objective(s) have been successfully met at the end of each class.

ON WINNING: Winning has to do with being successful or victorious in competitive events and in playing the games of life. Winners work to implement the goal-setting process, develop strategies and plans for making sure their objectives are met, and work out methods to be used in making their game plans a reality. The hallmark of all consistent winners is that they are fully cognizant of the boundaries, rules, prohibitions, penalties, set plays, and of the standards connected with game they choose to enter with whole heart. These also devote considerable time to the study of methods to improve their techniques, and to the practice of applications that are fundamental to winning on an individual basis and as a team player.

ON WORKING: Performing to produce or accomplish something requires that both mental and physical energy be directed toward the work; therefore, work should never be started without a clear understanding of what results are expected. Workers for pay have a responsibility for doing job assignments well at all times; therefore, they must know their jobs and be thoroughly familiar with both the equipment used and methods for troubleshooting equipment failures. In that they understand that their work will be graded or evaluated, wise persons take steps to clearly understand the evaluation criteria, and take pains to insure their performances meet or exceed expectations. These individuals also work closely with fellow workers and their supervisors in order to save time, effort, and resources.

ON WRITING: In that what and how one writes is sometimes used as an indicator of how neat, studious, and knowledgeable one tends to be, wise individuals take steps to insure their handwriting and typing chores are as flawless as possible in conveying their meanings, and that the rules of capitalization and punctuation are expertly applied in their compositions. Understanding that mastering paragraph development is the real key to writing well, they take steps to see that their ideas are presented skillfully. In addition, they keep a dictionary handy, use accepted writing formats, keep copies of papers that have been graded and critiqued, and maintain examples of properly written documents as guides for future writing chores.

ON YOU: Guide tips for being the best one can be include: know and be true to yourself; beware of false pride; know where you fit in; treat others as you would like to be treated, and special folk as they would like to be treated; discard bad habits and bad influences; know your limitations and your strengths and weaknesses; establish goals for not only realizing your dreams, but for minimizing or eliminating weaknesses that stem from one's prior conditioning; standardize procedures for all recurring activities; establish workable records-keeping systems; be courageous every day; be of good character and a good citizen; understand that great people make positive differences in the lives of others; copy the attributes of people you admire that can be adopted to fit within your personality and abilities; be open to making positive changes; and industriously collect and utilize tips for understanding and dealing with others, doing a job well, managing your resources, leading and loving others, and for being prosperous and happy. The degree to which you are committed to utilize these self-improvement guide tips, will in large measure determine the degree of success you will reach in being a better you.

REFERENCES

Aekin-Rothchild, Mary. *"To Scout or to Guide? The Girl Scout-Boy Scout Controversy."* Frontiers, A Journal of Women Studies. Nebraska Press, 1981.

Armstrong, Michelle. *Manage your Mind, Master your Life: How to Accelerate Your Success in Life and Business.* Santa Anna, California Seven Locks Press, 2006.

Beebe, Steven A., and Beebe, Susan J. *Public Speaking Handbook. Boston*: Allyn & Bacon Publishing, 2007.

Black, Howard and Black, Sandra. *Building Critical Thinking Skills for Reading, Writing, Math,* Seaside, California: Critical Thinking Books, 1998.

Bennis, Warren. *On Becoming A Leader.* Cambridge, MA: Perseus Publishing, 2003.

Bond, P. S. *Junior ROTC Manual.* Whitefish, Montana: Kessinger Publishing Company, 2007.

Butler, Gillian. *Managing Your Mind, Master Your Life: The Mental Fitness Guide.* New York: Oxford Press, 2007.

Bynam, Holland E., *"All-around Success In A Nutshell,"* E-book at allaroundsuccess.com., 2010.

------, *"Revelations In Glimpses From A Purpose-Filled Journey,"* E-book at holland bynam.com., 2011.

Certo, Samuel C. *Modern Management.* Upper Saddle River, New Jersey: Prentice Hall, 2002.

Goss, Jocelyn Pretlow. *Rhetoric & Readings For Writing.* Arlington, VA: Kendall-Hunt Publishing Company, 1975.

Haley, Alex. *The Autobiography of Malcolm X.* New York: Grove Press, 1965.

Harari, Oren. *The Leadership Secrets of Colin Powell.* New York: McGraw- Hill Companies, 2003.

Klavora, Peter and Chambers, Dave. *The Great Book of Inspiring Quotations: Motivational Sayings For All Occasions.* Tarentum, PA: Sports Book Publishers, 2001.

Kurtus, Ron and School For Champions LLC. *Failures of Abraham Lincoln.* Portland, OR: SFC Publishing Company, 2009.

London, Manuel. *Leadership Development: Paths to Self–Insight and Professional Growth.* Mahwah, NJ: Lawrence Erbaum Associates, 2001.

Martin, James, ed. *The Military Quotation Book.* New York: Saint Martin's Press, 1990. McArthur, John. *The Book On leadership.* Nashville, TN: Thomas Nelson, Inc., 2006.

Mount, M., Llies, R., & Johnson, E. (2006) "Relationship of Personality Traits and Counterproductive Work Behaviors: "The mediating effects of job satisfaction." *Personal Psychology*, 59, 591-622.

Oliva, Peter F. and Pawlas, George E. *Supervision For Today's Schools.* Hoboken, NJ*: Wiley*, John & Sons, *2007*.

Pink, Daniel H. *Drive, The Surprising Truth About What Motivates Us.* New York: Amazon Books, Dec. 29, 2001.

Parker, Jerome H, IV. "Fox Conner and Dwight Eisenhower: Mentoring and Application." (*Military Review*), July-August, 2005.

Powell, Colin L. *My American Journey.* New York: Random House, 1995.

Powell, Robert Baden. *Scouting For Boys: A Handbook For Instruction.* New York: Oxford University Press, Inc., 2004.

Skladany, Bob. *"Preparing for The Interview."* AARP, *The Magazine*, Dec.15, 2008.